How to Feel Good and How Not To

Also by John-Mark L. Miravalle
from Sophia Institute Press:

Beauty
What It Is and Why It Matters

JOHN-MARK L. MIRAVALLE

HOW TO
FEEL GOOD
and
HOW
NOT TO

The Ethics of Using Marijuana,
Alcohol, Antidepressants, and
Other Mood-Altering Drugs

SOPHIA INSTITUTE PRESS
Manchester, New Hampshire

Sophia Institute Press
Box 5284, Manchester, NH 03108
1-800-888-9344

www.SophiaInstitute.com

Sophia Institute Press® is a registered trademark of Sophia Institute.

Paperback ISBN 978-1-64413-086-5
eBook ISBN 978-1-64413-087-2

Library of Congress Control Number: 2020941561

First printing

Contents

Part 4

Moral Conclusions

How to Feel Good and How Not To

Part 1

Drugs and Feelings

1

The Dilemma of Drugs

Do you take drugs? Probably you do, sometimes. Alcohol is a drug. So is caffeine. Insulin and aspirin and allergy medications are all drugs. If you had an epidural while giving birth, you've been drugged.

This is fine, because a drug is simply anything that has some effect (besides nutrition or hydration) on the body or the mind when ingested. That's it.[1]

But probably some drugs you don't take. I'm guessing you don't make a habit of snorting cocaine or shooting up heroin or eating ecstasy. In fact, you probably think it's a bad idea for anybody to use those drugs.

But why? Do you think it's a bad idea because using those drugs is illegal and you can do jail time for it? Or because these drugs can do terrible things to your body, including kill you? Or because you're afraid you'll become addicted and you'll waste your life trying to get strung out as often as you can?

---

[1]   There's a lot of overlap between the terms "drug" and "poison," but the main thing to note is that *any* substance, whether food, drink, or drug, can, in certain doses and situations, be poisonous (i.e., harmful) to the body.

HOW TO FEEL GOOD and HOW NOT TO

Or is there a deeper reason why you think it's wrong to take these heavier, illegal drugs?

Why are people bothered by some drugs but not others? Is there a moral difference, or is it just a judgment call about the kind of risks you're willing to run?

Marijuana

Right now our nation is trying to make up its mind about using cannabis as a drug.

Cannabis is, as you probably know, a plant. You can use it to make rope, or fabric, or paper.[2] You can also employ the parts of the plant containing tetrahydrocannabinol (THC) — at which point the plant is commonly referred to as marijuana — as a drug. Marijuana can be ingested in a variety of ways, using a variety of accessories, and with a wide range of doses, concentrations, and effects.[3]

The short-term effects of marijuana include a pleasurable high, mood change, an altered sense of time, visual changes (e.g., colors appear brighter), and greater difficulty in movement, memory, and problem-solving.[4] Practical dangers associated with marijuana use include lung disease, driving accidents, and "cannabis use disorder, which has symptoms such as craving, withdrawal, lack of control, and negative effects on personal and professional responsibilities."[5]

---

[2] For the horticultural character and more common uses of cannabis, a helpful summary may be found in the first chapter of Martin Booth, *Cannabis: A History* (New York: Picador, 2003).

[3] Cannabis also contains cannabidiol (CBD), which is also employed as a drug in a variety of forms.

[4] See "Marijuana," National Institute on Drug Abuse, updated December 2019, https://www.drugabuse.gov/publications/drugfacts/marijuana.

[5] "Cannabis (Marijuana) and Cannabinoids: What You Need to Know," National Center for Complementary and Integrative Health,

Cannabis really made its presence felt in the Western world beginning in the nineteenth century, and in the twentieth century, many countries reacted by criminalizing its use as a drug in any context. But now a major reassessment is underway. Marijuana use has become extremely common — a 2016 telephone survey suggested that about half of Americans have used marijuana.[6] As of this writing, thirty-three states have legalized the sale of medical marijuana, and eleven states have made the sale of recreational marijuana legal.

Is this new trend of acceptance a good thing or not? People disagree, and for a lot of reasons — in fact, too many to enumerate here. Some of the pro-marijuana arguments emphasize that marijuana can make you feel good, can alleviate pain, and may have various physical and psychological benefits, and that the dangers to body or mind are relatively minor and infrequent. Opponents of the sale and use of marijuana will respond with counterstudies and counterexamples about the threats marijuana poses to body and mind. They worry that marijuana will lead to more car accidents, lung disease, and inactivity and will serve as a gateway to more harmful drug taking.

Who is right? And are these kinds of practical considerations really the best way to approach this issue? If so, shouldn't people just make their own calculations, their own prudential decisions about what potential risks they're willing to take in order to feel good?

---

last updated November 2019, https://www.nccih.nih.gov/health/cannabis-marijuana-and-cannabinoids-what-you-need-to-know.

[6] See Anthony Salvanto, Fred Backus, Jennifer De Pinto, and Sarah Dutton, "Marijuana Use and Support for Legal Marijuana Continue to Climb," CBS News, April 20, 2016, https://www.cbsnews.com/news/marijuana-use-and-support-for-legal-marijuana-continue-to-climb/.

HOW TO FEEL GOOD and HOW NOT TO

Because that's why people usually use marijuana: to feel good. And there's nothing wrong with wanting to feel good, is there? Or is there?

Alcohol

You can't have a discussion of mood-altering drugs without bringing in alcohol. This is the drug we all know, the drug we all take for granted. We share this drug with friends, with family, and even use it in our liturgical celebrations.

It has, of course, been around forever—but that doesn't mean it's somehow innocuous or benign.

The first time we hear about wine in the Bible is in the story of Noah: "Now Noah, a man of the soil, was the first to plant a vineyard. He drank some of the wine, became drunk, and lay naked inside his tent" (Gen. 9:20–21). So Noah, whom we rightly picture as the august patriarch, a figure of colossal importance, who preserved a remnant of animal and human life from the universal destruction of the deluge—this same Noah is here presented as stone-cold drunk, naked and passed out on the floor.

Alcohol has always had the power to do a lot of damage, to degrade and destroy people. Alcoholism causes broken relationships, unemployment, and despair. It can lead to horrible illnesses and is the third leading preventable cause of death in America.[7]

So we recognize the dangers of alcohol. America made drinking illegal for over a decade, and we still have relatively strict drinking-age laws compared with much of the rest of the world.

---

[7]   See A. H. Mokdad, J. S. Marks, D. F. Stroup, and J. L. Gerberding, "Actual Causes of Death in the United States 2000," *JAMA* 291, no. 10 (2004): 1238–1245.

And yet alcohol isn't really subject to the same kinds of moral concern and controversy. Most of us agree that you shouldn't drink and drive, that you shouldn't drink too much or too often, that you shouldn't try to drink all your problems away, and that alcoholism is a wretched condition that you should commit to fighting against in your life and in the lives of those you love.

Why, then, is marijuana such a hotly contested issue while alcohol isn't? Is it just that people in the Western world are prejudiced against an unfamiliar drug, but comfortable with beer and wine and whiskey because we've had them for so long? Is it because, as a society, we have a pretty straightforward set of ethical and behavioral rules when it comes to alcohol, but less so in the case of marijuana?

Or is there something else at stake?

Antidepressants

Is there any real difference between taking a drug to feel good and taking a drug to stop feeling bad?

Unlike "marijuana" or "alcohol," the term "antidepressants" doesn't denote a drug with a particular ingredient or derivation. These psychoactive drugs get their name not from a common origin but from a common use. They are psychopharmaceuticals that have been officially approved for use in treating depression and other common mood disorders.[8]

Early antidepressants included naturally occurring elements such as lithium and a variety of synthetically created medications (tricyclics and MAOIs) that were developed and used as antidepressants in the 1950s. These drugs were not originally designed to

---

[8] These drugs can also be prescribed for other, non-mood-related issues.

treat depression; their antidepressant potential was a purely "chance discovery."[9] In the 1980s, drugs with a different structure (the SSRIs, made famous by Prozac) took over the market, but a wide range of chemical treatments could still be prescribed for depressed patients.[10]

Today a lot of people take antidepressants. In 2010, antidepressants were the second most prescribed medication in the United States, with cholesterol medication in first place.[11] That means a lot of people are depressed. In fact, depression has been identified as the leading cause of medical disability in Canada and the United States.[12]

Depressed people feel terrible, and it's no wonder that the drugs have become so popular as a source of relief. But again, there has always been some controversy as to whether antidepressants are overprescribed and whether they really perform all that much better than placebos. Other concerns involve side effects, whether physical or psychological. What if it turned out that these drugs sometimes made you more miserable instead of less miserable?[13]

[9] See the preface to *Antidepressants: Past, Present, and Future*, ed. Sheldon H. Preskorn, John P. Feighner, Christina Y. Stanga, and Ruth Ross (Berlin: Springer-Verlag, 2004).

[10] For the definitive history of the rise of antidepressants, see David Healy, *The Antidepressant Era* (Cambridge, MA: Harvard University Press, 1997).

[11] See Thomas Insel, "Antidepressants: A Complicated Picture," National Institute of Mental Health, December 9, 2011, https://www.nimh.nih.gov/about/directors/thomas-insel/blog/2011/antidepressants-a-complicated-picture.shtml.

[12] See the *Global Burden of Disease* study put out by the World Health Organization in 2004: https://www.who.int/healthinfo/global_burden_disease/GBD_report_2004update_AnnexA.pdf.

[13] For instance, in 2017, GlaxoSmithKline, the original manufacturer of Paxil, was ordered to pay a three-million-dollar settlement to the widow of a man who committed suicide five days after going on the antidepressant. See Roni Caryn Rabin, "Lawsuit over a Suicide Points to a Risk of Antidepressants," *New York Times*,

Here again, the ethical discussion is often very practical. Do these drugs work? How well? Is the benefit usually worth the risk? But there are other, perhaps deeper questions to ask: What is depression? What is suffering generally? Does it mean anything or have any value? And if so, what meaning? What value?

Getting a sense of the answers to those questions might be the best way to start looking at how to approach the issue of antidepressants in our culture.

This Book

These three groups of drugs—marijuana products, alcoholic drinks, and antidepressants—all share an important feature: they all have a pronounced effect on how you feel.

They are also incredibly widespread and influential.

This book is about helping to make clear, consistent, moral judgments about these drugs—that is to say, when and whether using them to change your feelings is a good idea.

But to do that, we'll have to look at what feelings are. Why do we feel good? Why do we feel bad? What does it matter?

This book is intended to address the phenomenon of chemical mood alteration. But it's also meant to be a reflection on our feelings of pleasure and suffering and how those relate to the rest of our humanity.

When we realize the way we're made to exist, and why we have emotions in the first place, it should give us not only a better perspective from which to evaluate different kinds of drug use but also a framework that will enable us to better cultivate an emotional life that leads to happiness and fulfillment.

September 11, 2017, https://www.nytimes.com/2017/09/11/well/mind/paxil-antidepressants-suicide.html.

2

The Body and Human Feeling

When I was doing research on the morality of using drugs to affect feelings, over a decade and a half ago, I made an appointment with a local (Christian) mental health professional. I asked him what he thought our feelings were for.

I remember very clearly how he answered my question.

He said, "Our feelings aren't *for* anything. They're just there. There's no rhyme or reason to them."

So I asked him what we were supposed to do with them.

"Manage them," he said.

Now, if you think that—if you think the emotions are random and meaningless and that you just have to "deal with them" any way you can—then there's not much more to say. There won't be any rules or guidelines one way or another, and we will each have to do our best to get our feelings to a place that we, personally, find acceptable.

But that's not the only way to think about our feelings. And before we talk about drugs that target our feelings, it would be wise to consider a more robust account of the emotions—one that offers a detailed picture of what feelings are *and* what they are for.

HOW TO FEEL GOOD and HOW NOT TO

The best presentation of the feelings (or "passions," as they're traditionally called)[14] that I know is the one given by St. Thomas Aquinas.[15] According to him, our passions or feelings are *our reactions toward what we perceive as being good (and therefore pleasing), and away from what we perceive as being bad (and therefore displeasing).*

The idea is pretty straightforward. If we perceive something as bad, we don't like it and are repelled by it. If we perceive something as good, we like it and are attracted to it. The passions, then, are these felt movements toward what we like and away from what we don't like.

Within these two categories — movements toward what we like and away from what we don't — is the subdivision of the basic passions.[16] It includes feelings such as liking, disliking, desire, repugnance, enjoying, and suffering.

There are also feelings for times when getting what you like or avoiding what you don't becomes difficult. In these more demanding situations, the emotions of hope, despair, anger, fear, and courage propel you toward and away from various things that you experience as being good or bad.[17]

This is a profoundly helpful layout of human feeling, but for our purposes it's probably sufficient to point out the centrality of

---

14 I'll also use the terms "emotions," "drives," and "impulses" interchangeably with "passions" and "feelings."

15 And adopted, in simplified form, by the *Catechism of the Catholic Church* (CCC), nos. 1762–1775.

16 Also called the *concupiscible* passions.

17 With this more complicated set of *irascible* passions, you can either classify them by the perceived good or evil they're responding to (hope and despair respond to a perceived good, fear and daring and anger respond to a perceived evil), or by whether they prompt the person to approach or with withdraw from the object (despair and fear prompt a withdrawal, whereas hope and despair and anger prompt an approach). See St. Thomas Aquinas, *Summa theologiae* (*ST*), I-II, q. 23, a. 2.

suffering and enjoyment. The passions are our impulses, and every impulse is ultimately directed toward the experience of delightful things and the avoidance of unpleasant things. Aquinas states that "joy and sadness are said to be principal because in them all the other passions have their completion and end."[18]

So every time you feel something, that feeling centers on something that can give you pleasure or something that can give you displeasure. All your emotions, all your passions, are about being pulled toward something you experience as good (which can cause you *enjoyment*) or away from something you experience as bad (which can cause you to *suffer*).

Now if you can make a person feel delight with a drug, or not feel sorrow with a drug, that's very significant for the rest of a person's emotional life. You can essentially reorient all of a person's feelings based on the promise of attaining pleasure and avoiding suffering—since, as we just said, all the other feelings are geared toward those two goals.

So could drugs be the final fulfillment of the entire emotional life of a person?

Feelings and the Human Body

We could explore a huge range of topics connected to the passions, but for our discussion of mood-altering drugs, the two areas to hone in on are (a) the way we experience our passions physically and (b) the way we experience them morally.

Human feelings are generally associated with some physiological change.[19] When you feel something, you tend to feel it in your

---

[18] Ibid., I-II, q. 25, a. 4.
[19] "Passion is properly to be found where there is corporeal transmutation." *ST*, I-II, q. 23, a. 3.

flesh. Anger, desire, fear, joy, sorrow—in all these cases, we can notice our breathing changing, our heart speeding up or calming down, our skin tingling—and scientific instruments can detect a host of chemical and neurological changes that happen when our feelings go through some significant shift.

But are the emotions *just* physical? Are they just biological processes? Certainly our whole discussion of drugs and feelings is based on the assumption that it's possible to change how we feel by introducing various chemical stimulants into our bodies. Does that mean that our feelings are nothing more than chemical occurrences?

Not at all. Yes, there is a physical aspect of feeling, but there's definitely a nonphysical component as well. We realize this as soon as we try to imagine something purely material having a feeling.

Pick anything purely material—say, a glass marble. That marble can't feel pain or pleasure. And it doesn't matter how many marbles you pile up, or how ingeniously you arrange the pile, the group of marbles will never be able to feel pleasure or pain, since, after all, the group of marbles is just as inanimate as the individual marbles that constitute it.

You can run the same thought experiment with any other merely material substance: nails or grains of sand or molecules or subatomic particles. If something is made up of nothing but matter, it can't have a felt experience. And if you look at the human body, or at the body of any animal, merely in terms of its elemental materials, you'll see that it's composed of the same lifeless bits of stuff as everything else in the physical universe. This means the body by itself can't be what's experiencing pleasure or pain.[20]

---

[20] This also explains why it makes sense to say that even the lower animals have a soul—not a spiritual soul but some immaterial principle that allows them to have genuine feelings. Animals

Here's another illustration of the same point. My kids, when they're young, will sometimes sit in a certain position too long, and when they try to move again, they find their foot has gone to sleep. It feels weird, and then it feels painful as sensation returns. My young children know this feeling and complain about it when it happens. But they have no idea what the underlying physical causes of this feeling are. They know nothing about circulation. They haven't heard the term "blood vessel," and at first they don't even make the connection between the sitting position and the subsequent pain.

The point is that my kids *do* know what it feels like to have their foot go to sleep, but they *don't* know the physiological causes or correlates that go with that feeling. So they know the feeling, but not the body state; and if they can know one, but not the other, it proves that the two are different. Body states (e.g., diminished blood circulation) and soul states (e.g., feeling your foot go to sleep) may be correlated in the human person, but they aren't the same thing, even in the case of physical pain. The pain is in the soul, even if it's caused by the body and has physical manifestations.[21]

The immateriality of passion is even more apparent when our feelings are responses to properly immaterial objects. One of my favorite examples is the fear of public speaking. In this case, the physical symptoms are usually pretty clear (and inconvenient): sweaty palms, trembling knees, shaky voice. But what exactly is

---

clearly have passions: they like things and dislike things and feel pain and pleasure accordingly, which means they can't be reduced to simply their chemical makeup.

[21] "We speak of pain of the body because the cause of pain is in the body: as when we suffer something hurtful to the body. But the movement of pain is always in the soul; since 'the body cannot feel pain unless the soul feel it,' as Augustine says." *ST*, I-II, q. 35, a. 1, ad. 1.

the prospective speaker scared of? Is he worried that if he does a poor job, the audience will throw things, or bite him, or deny him food? Clearly not: he's not afraid of any physical threat at all. He's afraid of the immaterial evil of shame, of being perceived by others—and maybe by oneself—as holding little interest, or worth.

The same happens in the case of emotional reactions to immaterial goods. If the audience applauds enthusiastically at the end of the talk, the speaker will likely be delighted, and the delight might cause a thrill to run through his whole body. But it's not because the actual noise of handclaps is somehow physically pleasurable—nobody listens to recordings of clapping in the car or doing dishes at home. It's because the applause is a sign of something immaterial: success, appreciation, the achievement of mutual understanding and sympathy—which feels great.

Aquinas distinguishes *bodily passion*, which starts in the body and ends in the soul (such as your foot's going to sleep), from *psychical passion*, which starts in the soul and ends in the body (such as the fear of public speaking).[22] In both cases, you have something physical happening as well as a movement of the soul. But more importantly, feelings can be triggered by physical causes or by psychological causes, and so to understand a given emotion requires trying to find out where that emotion originated.

A feeling might have its origins in a body state or in a soul state. You might feel giddy because you just ate a ton of sugar or because the love of your life just proposed to you. You might feel unable to take pleasure in anything because you have had hardly any sleep for a week straight or because your spouse just passed away.

So people have to be really careful not to overspiritualize, or overmaterialize, their feelings. Not every bad feeling is the result of some interior struggle: it could be largely due to poor diet and

---

[22] *De veritate*, q. 26, a. 2.

a lack of exercise. And not every bad feeling comes from some chemical imbalance: it could be largely due to vicious living and an absence of purpose. We're a body-soul composite, and unless we respect that truth about ourselves, we won't know how to make sense of our passions.

Some human feelings have material causes, and some have immaterial causes. This fundamental fact about the sources of feelings will prove significant in our later evaluation of drugs that alter feelings.

The Right Feeling at the Right Time

If there's one thing that anyone with a little common sense can recognize, it's that sometimes our feelings are misdirected. Sometimes we're inclined toward what we know is wrong and away from what we know is right. We desire too much food, more food than we know is good for us. We enjoy hurting people who unintentionally offend us. We dislike exercise. We're averse to prayer and try to avoid it. We hope to gain satisfaction through money, and we fear commitment.

That's why most people realize that good and evil, right and wrong, do not correspond to pleasure and pain. Our feelings, our inclinations, are not the basis for what's moral and what isn't, since our drives are sometimes disordered—i.e., they pull us the wrong way. This proclivity for our passions to be disordered is called *concupiscence*.

What then, should our attitude toward our own feelings be? We might adopt an extremist position, condemning all passions as evil or celebrating them all as good. Let's call these the *stoic* and *epicurean* positions, respectively, since, as Aquinas notes, "While some of the Stoics maintained that all pleasures are evil, the Epicureans held that pleasure is good in itself, and that consequently all pleasures are good."[23] Both of these positions turn out to be badly misconstrued.

The stoic position encourages the elimination of the emotional life. On this view, all our feelings and urges are temptations, or at least distractions from what really matters. In this case, the right response to strong emotions is to neutralize them.

What would be the implications of stoicism for drug use? Simple. If you're supposed to repress feeling as much as possible, then presumably drugs should be used to the extent that they diminish feeling of any kind. Drugs could be used to flatten people out emotionally, to eliminate any powerful emotion.

However, if the passions are an essential feature of being human, then to attack the passions is to attack our humanity. Presumably, then, it would be better to help the different facets of our nature to flourish rather than target them for repression. Just as integral health requires that every part of the body function, so, too, integral psychological health requires that every part of the soul—including the passions—work as it was made to. The passions are good, with a God-given purpose. They shouldn't be repressed or dismissed.

Alternately, the epicurean position maintains that the key to life consists in cultivating very forceful desires and satisfying them as best we can. It essentially recommends handing the reins over to our passions and letting them direct all our decisions, since the measure of good is what feels good.

Here again, the implications for drug use would be obvious: if the epicurean approach is right, chemicals that give intense pleasures should be used liberally. If we're here just to feel good, and if these drugs can get you to feel really, really good, then the conclusion is straightforward: enjoy the drugs. Pick the ones that

[23] *ST*, I-II, q. 34, a. 2.

provide the greatest amount of pleasure and result in the least amount of unpleasantness.

But of course the epicurean attitude is wrong too. The passions can't by themselves guide our behavior because our passions themselves are in conflict. I may have a desire both to eat indulgently and to stay fit, but I know that satisfying the first desire will prevent satisfying the second. So I'll have to choose between them—but then how will I choose? Clearly, I'll have to look for some principle that goes beyond the passions if I'm going to judge between them.

In sum: our feelings, which are a kind of psychosomatic propulsion system, exist to propel us toward what's good for us and away from what's bad for us—but our feelings themselves don't necessarily tell us which is which. That means if we're going to encourage certain feelings and discourage others, it should be on the basis of some other standard—namely, what's good for us and what isn't.

Since we're looking at drugs that stimulate some feelings and diminish others, our assessment of these drugs will have to be based on whether the feelings these drugs produce or reduce are a good fit with our nature.

What that means is that we'll have to look at the kinds of pleasures produced by marijuana and alcohol and see if they're good pleasures.

And we'll have to look at the kinds of sufferings reduced by antidepressants and see whether they're bad sufferings.

Then we'll know what kind of drug use is good for us and what kind isn't.

Part 2

Drugs Taken to Produce Pleasure

3

Recreation and the Pleasures of the Psyche

The phrase "recreational drug use" may have a pejorative association for most people, but it's not immediately clear why that should be the case. After all, recreation isn't necessarily a bad or trivial thing. In fact, depending on how we define "recreation," it may turn out to be one of the most important pursuits there is.

Suppose we define it like this: *recreation is a break from working for physical self-support in order to turn to activities that stimulate and delight the soul or mind.*

On this definition, recreation (or leisure) is supremely important. By it, we attempt to fulfill our full humanity, instead of just focusing on money, food, shelter, or the other things necessary for survival.

So, if we're going to look at recreational marijuana and recreational (i.e., alcoholic) beverages, we should probably try to get a clear picture of what the basic pursuit of recreation looks like.

What are people generally looking for when they ingest marijuana or alcohol? What satisfactions of the soul or mind does recreation offer?

Recreation and Rest

The first point to notice is that recreation is closely tied to an attitude of restfulness. In fact, the very experience of delight itself is tied to rest.

HOW TO FEEL GOOD and HOW NOT TO

On Aquinas's reading, all the emotions, except one, prompt or dispose the subject to move. They stimulate, motivate, precipitate change. The single exception is delight.[24] Delight may motivate action by its absence—when once you've tasted delight, you'll do an awful lot to get it back again—but when delight is present, its only demand is that you rest.[25]

Sorrow, which we'll discuss later in greater depth, is the response to something experienced as evil, and it clamors that somebody do something to fix the situation. Delight is the response to something experienced as good, and it invites repose in that good.[26] It says, "This is a good place to be. Let's stay here."

The implication is that recreation and its attendant delight are founded on a commitment to *rest*.

And that means that if you can't or won't rest, you're not going to be able to recreate. And a lot of people have a hard time resting,

---

[24] Even the feeling of despair, it turns out, "implies a movement of withdrawal" from a difficult good. See *ST*, I-II, q. 40, a. 4.

[25] A note on terminology: although I think it's possible to use "joy" and "delight" and "pleasure" synonymously, the sometimes vastly different connotations these words carry might make it confusing to switch back and forth between them indiscriminately. For instance, while joy might have a spiritual, edifying association ("She was a virtuous, joy-filled person"), pleasure can sometimes sound base or low ("All he cares about is pleasure") or even evil ("He took a twisted pleasure in getting revenge"). So I'll mostly use the word "delight" (and sometimes "enjoyment") to mean the felt response to something perceived as good—whether it's a physical good perceived through the senses, a spiritual good perceived at the level of the soul, or something good perceived at both levels simultaneously. But just be aware that sometimes the sources I cite will use "joy" or "pleasure" and mean the same thing I mean by "delight."

[26] "Pleasure is the repose of the appetite in good." *ST*, I-II, q. 34, a. 2, ad. 3.

letting go, just being.[27] When there's so much to do, so much to get done, people run the risk of failing in the core responsibility of delight. And it is a responsibility, at least for Christians. It's an obligation explicitly delineated in the third commandment. Apparently, rest is so foreign, so unlikely for human beings to pursue on their own, that God needs to give us a direct order to take some time every week and prepare for heaven by resting with Him. If left to themselves, people will prefer the merciless yoke of productivity to the joy of the Lord.

Now, if rest means detachment from work, from *doing*, it also means an emphasis on *being*. Delight is repose in the good, but because, in reality, being and truth and goodness are interchangeable, delight can also be described as a celebration of being. God rested because He saw that all that He had made was "very good." So, too, our rest is meant to be a celebration of reality. It's a celebration of all creation.

Unfortunately, there are two addictions that prevent us from rest and its attendant delight. One is workaholism. If you're addicted to doing, to producing, you won't be able to rest and celebrate being. But the other enemy of rest is idleness. If rest means a celebration of reality, idleness is a restless attempt to *escape* reality. Picture a bored guy on a couch, flipping channels frantically, trying to find a moment of entertainment that can make him forget what his world is actually like.[28]

---

[27] As Pope St. Paul VI, in his exhortation on Christian joy, worries that for many people, "the burden of their charges, in a fast-moving world, too often prevents them from enjoying daily joys." *Gaudete in Domino* (May 9, 1975), no. 5.

[28] As Josef Pieper points out, Aquinas interprets idleness as a sin against the third commandment. It's not fostering delight in creation. It's not a restful state of mind. *Leisure: The Basis of Culture*, trans. Alexander Dru (San Francisco: Ignatius Press, 2009), 45.

HOW TO FEEL GOOD and HOW NOT TO

For many people, life is nothing more than a miserable vacillation between these two states. People go to jobs where they slave away without seeing any ultimate purpose to their work and then come home and binge on Netflix. Then they go back to work, if only to escape the dullness of their entertainment. Josef Pieper cites an author who perfectly captures this hellish incapacity for joy: "One must work, if not from taste then at least from despair. For, to reduce everything to a single truth: work is less boring than pleasure."[29]

How does one escape from this vicious cycle of productivity and entertainment? By stepping back, slowing down, and learning to rest in the goodness of things. That's, ultimately, what recreation is all about.

But hold on: Isn't that what recreational marijuana use is all about? Stepping back, slowing down, and learning to rest in the goodness of things?

Certainly that sounds, at least initially, like what people are going for when they smoke weed.

Contemplative Delight

Another one of the chief delights traditionally associated with recreation is one of contemplation. Again, when we take a break from worrying about the body, we can focus our attention on mental activities. To put it differently, when we cut back on doing, we can devote some time to reflection.

Later, when we talk about sorrow and depression, we'll talk about the importance of finding legitimate sources of delight to counteract sadness at any level. Aquinas, in fact, enumerates a variety of delightful remedies for pain and sorrow. But no other remedy receives so strong an endorsement as does contemplation:

---

[29] Pieper, *Leisure*, 69.

As stated above, the greatest of all pleasures consists in the contemplation of truth. Now every pleasure assuages pain as stated above: hence the contemplation of truth assuages pain or sorrow, and the more so the more perfectly one is a lover of wisdom. And therefore in the midst of tribulations men rejoice in the contemplation of Divine things and of future Happiness.[30]

It's a pretty tall order trying to convince people today that contemplation of truth is delightful, let alone that it's the greatest delight there is. Nonetheless, I think it is the case. The mind longs to know things as the stomach wants food. And since the mind is incalculably more sophisticated than the stomach, the satisfaction of knowing should be proportionately higher than the satisfaction of having a full belly.

Knowing individual facts (sport stats, random dates, bits of gossip) can be pleasant, but not sufficient, like having an appetizer and no dinner. But big ideas, ideas that put everything in a new light — there's food for the soul! Think about the last time a talk or a book or even a movie "blew your mind." Probably it wove together large pieces of your experience — stuff that you knew already — and connected them to some larger principle in a way that brought it all together. Maybe it has been a while for you, but there's nothing like it. We gain our knowledge piecemeal, and when we're able to put the pieces together into a coherent picture, it's enormously gratifying:

A sense of altitude awes but also thrills the soul of the [intellectual] worker; he is like the mountaineer amid rocks and glaciers. The world of ideas opens up scenes more sublime than those of the Alpine landscape, and they fill him with

[30] *ST*, I-II, q. 38, a. 5.

rapture.... According to the Angelic Doctor, contemplation begins in love and ends in joy.[31]

The desire for knowledge is a constant feature of human life, and the information age has developed countless options for intellectual pleasure in the form of blogs, quiz shows, talk shows, social media sites, Siri, *Wikipedia*, TED talks, gossipy magazines, podcasts, and so forth. People go to these sources to fight boredom—but boredom can be fought only with enjoyment. This means that knowing things is enjoyable. Knowledge is "stimulating," entertaining, interesting. It's delightful just to know.

The problem, of course, is that these examples are incredibly lazy, unreliable ways of getting knowledge, and low-grade knowledge at that. Another tragic example can be taken from the people who feel "well informed" because they watch an hour or so of news every night. News stations are expert at providing clever substitutes for actual wisdom. Not only do they sensationalize disconnected pieces of information, but they even provide an overarching structure for interpreting everything (e.g., for one news provider, everything can be explained by the principle "conservatives are selfish and evil," and for another news provider, everything can be explained by the principle "liberals are stupid and evil"). Thus news junkies can come to think that they're aware of and understand everything worth knowing—even if they've literally never spent *one minute's* energy on rigorous consideration or honest research regarding the ultimate things.

What's really satisfying is thinking about the central existential issues, the comprehensive ideas, the core principles of existence and human life.

[31] A. G. Sertillanges, O.P., *The Intellectual Life: Its Spirit, Conditions, Methods*, trans. Mary Ryan (Washington, DC: Catholic University of America, 1998), 255.

But again, couldn't marijuana use help with that? When people stay up really late, or have a couple drinks, or share a joint with friends, it seems, somehow, to encourage reflection on the important things. Big questions surface more easily: Why are we here? What's the point of everything? What should I do with my life?

So could marijuana use actually be an aid to the mind's pursuit of ultimate truth?

The Delight of Community

The final aspect of recreation—of satisfying the soul—that I want to touch on in this chapter is community.

There's a connection between recreation and celebration, and I think we usually associate celebration as being with other people. It can be sad, for instance, to spend holidays alone, or to go to a movie or a sporting event by yourself.

Being in relationship with others, and more, loving people, allows you to experience their good as a good for you and their evil as your own misfortune. This raises the stakes: another self is an amplifier for your own experience of both joy and sorrow. For instance, when someone you really love is in pain, it's torturous—much worse than anything you've ever been through on your own.

And yet nothing compares to the soul's delight in love. When someone you love is happy—and better yet, when that person is happy because of something you did—there's no feeling like it. Making a good friend laugh, watching the excitement of a child you care about, the delight you can give to a spouse: these are the best moments life has to offer. Absolutely the best.

Here, too, I think most users of recreational drugs would endorse the above characterization of the importance of love and relationship. And certainly recreational drugs—as well as recreational beverages—are frequently partaken of in communal settings. You go to a bar to drink with other people, and you bring beer to a barbecue and wine to dinner at a friend's house. Similarly, people pass the joint around the bonfire, and the bong around the living room. One of the most common justifications I hear for recreational marijuana use is that it lowers social inhibitions and promotes sociability. And there's no denying that marijuana users—especially those associated with hippie-type movements—spend a lot of time talking (and singing!) about the centrality of love.

So could smoking weed make you a more loving, other-centered person?

Summary

The point of this chapter has been to highlight the good of recreation and explore the ways in which recreational marijuana users seem to be—as the term for their activity implies—pursuing a kind of recreational activity, i.e., something that can help fulfill and delight the soul.

Although we certainly haven't enumerated every kind of leisure (we'll talk about aesthetic appreciation in a later chapter, for instance), I think this is a good framework within which to assess whether recreational drug use is genuine recreation. Recreation involves a celebration of being (*rest*), of truth (*contemplation*), and of the goodness of others (*love*).

If recreational drug use entails an achievement of these goods, so much the better. If not, it will be that much more difficult to justify it.

4

Marijuana and Deceptive Experience

Our analysis of feelings and the edifying delight of recreation should by now be an adequate context for talking intelligently about recreational drug use. Can smoking weed assist us in celebrating being, truth, and goodness? Can it contribute to our overall happiness?

When I was in college, I saw a comedy film in which one of the main characters was throwing darts in a bar. At one point he was jostled in the middle of a throw, which messed up his aim so that he threw the dart into the back of a patron's head. The guy with the dart in his head blinked a couple of times and said, "I taste ice cream." His companion looked at him and said, essentially, "You've got a dart in your head, you dumb goof."

Because, of course, the guy wasn't really tasting ice cream. He was having a taste hallucination as the result of an artificial intervention in his brain. What happened to him is what happens in every hallucination: the person senses things that aren't there. One of my friends used to be pretty heavily into drugs, and he told me how once, after secretly dropping acid while riding in a car with a friend, he turned to look at the driver and saw a massive turtle eating popcorn. The turtle turned to him and said, "Are you okay, man? You look weird."

Now, obviously, my friend didn't really see a giant humanoid turtle driving the car—because there *are* no giant humanoid turtles who can drive. My friend, the dumb goof, had a chemical dart in his head.

And if we don't think drug-induced hallucinations give us real perceptual objects, why should we think that other drug-induced experience gives us real insights? Take, for instance, the spiritualistic claims made on behalf of psychedelics, or "entheogens"—literally, "God within"—as they're increasingly called. People report encounters with God, visions of ultimate truth, and major mystical and metaphysical insights. Michael Pollan has recently written about how "the extraordinary promise on offer in the Church of Psychedelics is that anyone at any time may gain access to the primary religious experience by means of the sacrament, which happens to be a psychoactive molecule. Faith is rendered superfluous."[32]

It seems very plain to me that we should say to these people what was said to the guy who thought he tasted ice cream: "You've got a dart in your head, you dumb goof." Tripping on LSD or psilocybin isn't really engaging the divine any more than my friend was really seeing a massive turtle next to him in the driver's seat. In both cases, the brain was artificially stimulated to produce artificial experiences. Drugs can *simulate*, but they can't *produce*, genuine perceptions or insights.

And what's true about sensations and mystical insights also holds good for feelings. Drugs can simulate delight, they can create an artificial sense of delight, they can make you think you're having delight—but they can't give you delight. All they can give you is an emotional hallucination or deceptive pleasure.

Not all delight is true delight: "just as it happens that not every good which is desired is of itself and verily good, so not every

[32] Michael Pollan, *How to Change Your Mind: What the New Science of Psychedelics Teaches Us about Consciousness, Dying, Addiction, Depression, and Transcendence* (New York: Penguin, 2018), 26.

pleasure is of itself and verily good."[33] An experience that simulates feeling good, but without being a response to an actual good, isn't a good feeling. If delight is the proper human response to perceiving a real good, then artificially mimicking such feelings independently of a perceived good could be called counterfeit, or bogus, or deceptive delight. That's, I think, what we're looking at when it comes to the recreational use of marijuana.

Deceptive Delight

The essence of delight is *a response to union with a good, which prompts the person to rest in that good.* Recreational drug use is very different: it's an attempt to *achieve an enjoyable brain state, which prompts the person to rest in that brain state.* To reiterate: delight is a response to something truly good, whereas drug-induced experience is simply a response to a deliberately stimulated state of the brain.

It's easy to find analogies on the physical level. Let's go back to the ice cream example. Suppose some guy had managed to figure out how to enjoy the taste of ice cream by poking the back of his skull with a needle, and whenever other people were enjoying dessert, he sat there at the table repeatedly sticking himself in the head. I'm pretty sure everyone else at the table would recognize that something unhealthy was going on.

Or take the more realistic case of sexual delight on the physical level, which is meant to be experienced as a response to the objective goodness of union with one's spouse. Masturbation, by contrast, doesn't care about the objective good; it just wants a particular feeling and so manipulates the body to get that feeling. So, too, recreational drug use doesn't care about the objective good;

---

[33] St. Thomas Aquinas, *ST*, I-II, q. 34, a. 2, ad. 3.

it just wants a particular feeling and so manipulates the body to get that feeling.

These examples illustrate a key principle: "Pleasure that is sought for itself becomes unwholesome."[34] When delight becomes its own object—when we want to feel good just because we want to feel good—then our feelings turn in on themselves, like eyes flipped backward in the head. That can't be authentic. Authentic delight can only be a response, a reaction, to something beyond the feeling itself.

Put differently, in the case of drug-induced experiences, the mental faculty is not responding to the object to which it was designed to respond. It's not enough, humanly speaking, for what you think or see or feel to be in response to any reality—it has to be in response to the reality that is the proper object of that faculty. If you think you see stars because you took a blow to the head, your visual capacity is responding to the wrong reality—namely, the shock to the brain. Your visual capacity isn't responding to the reality it's meant to respond to—namely, the surrounding visible environment—which is why what you see isn't real. It's fake, or deceptive.

And it's not even enough, humanly speaking, for your experience to *correspond to* reality. It has to be *caused by* the reality that is its proper object. Let me give an example. In Oscar Wilde's famous play *The Importance of Being Earnest*, Gwendolyn believes that her fiancé is named Earnest. She thinks this because he has told her that his name is Earnest, even though he thinks his name is Jack. At the conclusion of the play, we discover that his name *was* Earnest all along, because, as it happens, his long-lost birth parents had given him the very name he was coincidentally using as an alias.

---

[34] Pontifical Council for Health Pastoral Care, *Church: Drugs and Drug Addiction* (November 1, 2001), no. 317.

Now notice this strange thing: Gwendolyn believes something that is true (namely, that her fiancé's name is Earnest), but she's also being lied to! Why? Because even though her belief *corresponds to* the reality or fact that Earnest's name is Earnest, it's not *caused by* that reality or fact. It's caused by Earnest's desire to misrepresent things.[35] She believed the right thing for the wrong reason.

So, too, recreational drug use has the potential to make people feel the right way but for the wrong reason. We spent the last chapter talking about how good reality is, how delightful being and truth and goodness are. Delight is the proper response to the world, sure enough. But cannabis can't help people feel the way they should feel because even if feeling good is appropriate to the situation, they should feel it as the result of actually perceiving the goodness of things. If they feel delight as a result of chemically manipulating the brain, their experience may correspond to reality in some way, but it won't be conformed to reality. Like Gwendolyn's belief, a drug user's pleasure is deceptive down to its roots.[36]

Again, delight is designed to be a response to the goodness of being and truth and other people. But the pleasure of pot smoking is a response to an intoxicating plant (technically classed as a hallucinogen). Therefore, the pleasure of recreational drug use

---

[35] See Edmund L. Gettier's famous article showing that "justified, true belief" does not necessarily count as knowledge. "Is Justified True Belief Knowledge?" *Analysis* 23 (1963): 121–123.

[36] "In a way, drugs have become the indicator of a society which, instead of proposing the values of life, encourages escape into a pleasant and *deceptive state of euphoria*, attainable through the use of drugs.... As we have repeated several times, the drug addict makes use of products or drugs with the purpose of attaining *deceptive pleasure and happiness*, above all in order to reassure him or herself." Pontifical Council for Health Pastoral Care, *Church: Drugs and Drug Addiction*, nos. 261, 274, emphasis mine.

is "deceptive" insofar as it mimics the joys that are proper to the human condition.

Immaterial Delight and Drug Use

I said in the last chapter that genuine recreation is geared not so much to the satisfactions of the body as to the satisfactions of the soul. I also said two chapters ago that some feelings (including some delights) are responses to immaterial objects.

The deep goodness of existence, the nonnecessity of the world and yourself, the inner joy of another person, the ultimate significance and purpose of human life—none of these sources of recreational joy are things you can touch or taste or see or hear.

The soul or mind is an invisible, immaterial thing, and it engages these immaterial realities. The brain is a visible, physical thing. It doesn't engage these realities, and messing with it chemically won't make it engage these realities better.

Consequently, immaterial delight and genuine recreation can't be brought about by a change to the body, because the brain is not responsible for these acts—the soul is. In other words, the spiritual causes of joy aren't material, since they're not accessible to the senses.

True, the soul does *rely* on the proper functioning of the brain to carry out its higher spiritual functions. But that just means that although the brain can't *cause* the mind to function properly, it can *prevent* the mind from functioning properly. That's why a description of the physical state of your brain can't explain why your mind is working rightly, but it can explain why your mind is working wrongly.

For instance, if a teacher asks a student, "Sally, explain to me how you knew that six times six equals thirty-six," it wouldn't be a good answer for Sally to say, "Because my neurons are firing at a normal rate and in a normal pattern." The teacher doesn't want to know about Sally's *brain state*; the teacher wants to know about Sally's *mental processes*—and the two are not the same thing. The right workings of the mind, not the right workings of the brain, are the only adequate explanation for truth or goodness or wholesome delight.

That's why even a drug that helps people focus on discursive-reasoning tasks—as in the case, say, of Paul Erdős, who kept himself on a standard regimen of amphetamines to increase his prodigious mathematical output—isn't the cause of any acquired insight. Instead we could say that such a drug only facilitates one mental function by suppressing another that might be distracting to the first. The drug, in other words, would make it easier to be open to reality in one way by making the mind less responsive in another. This could explain why people like Erdős, who became so artificially adept in one area of human life, can be so clueless in other areas.

On the other hand, a mind's malfunction might be explicable in terms of a brain update. If the teacher asks a student, "Bobby, explain to me why you wrote that six times six equals Milwaukee," it could be a legitimate excuse for Bobby to say, "I'm so sorry. I didn't get any sleep last night, and I fell on the stairs and hit my head right before coming into class this morning. My head is swimming, and I didn't know what I was doing during the test."

If there were some cerebral malfunctioning, as in the above scenario, it's conceivable that a medication might *enable* thought by somehow fixing a problem in the brain. That wouldn't, of course, guarantee that the mind would work right, but only that the physical conditions for its proper operation would have been restored. Caffeine can't produce good thinking, but it can remove the obstacle to good thinking, which is the body's fatigue.

So, apart from a medication for a clear physiological issue, the metaphysical principle remains: an intervention in the brain can't make your soul work right, but it can distort, destabilize or inhibit your thoughts and feelings. This is precisely how recreational cannabis works: it is used to affect the brain in such a way that the soul's grasp on reality is loosened. Joseph Ratzinger states the matter very vividly:

> I would put it this way: drugs are a form of protest against facts. The one who takes them refuses to resign himself to the world of facts. He seeks a better world. Drugs are the result of despair in a world experienced as a dungeon of facts, in which man cannot hold out for long. Naturally, many other things are involved, too: the search for adventure; the conformity of joining in what others are doing; the cleverness of the dealers, and so on. But the core is a protest against a reality perceived as a prison.... Drugs are the pseudo-mysticism of a world that does not believe yet cannot get rid of the soul's yearning for paradise.[37]

I get why people smoke weed recreationally. The reason is very simple: we need delight, and not just physical pleasure but real psychological joy. The human person was made for the joy of being, of truth, of goodness. We can't do without it.

And no human being can long remain pleasureless and sad.... And the Philosopher accordingly says in the *Ethics* that those who cannot enjoy spiritual pleasures turn their endeavors for the most part to bodily pleasures. And so due to the sadness conceived regarding spiritual goods, their minds then wander over the illicit things in which the carnal spirit takes pleasure.[38]

---

[37] Joseph Ratzinger, A *Turning Point for Europe?* trans. Brian McNeil (San Francisco: Ignatius Press, 2010), 25–26.
[38] St. Thomas Aquinas, *De malo*, q. 11, a. 4.

The upshot is that to the extent that people don't know how to find delight in the world as it is, they often — in their despair — attempt to manufacture enjoyable feelings by manipulating their own faculties. Recreational marijuana use is one such attempt.

5

Real versus Counterfeit Delight

I've basically made two points about what people are trying to do in the case of recreational drug use, and in particular the recreational use of marijuana. First, I've claimed that people are motivated by a desire for delight, and in particular the delights of rest and contemplation and love. These are real human goods—they are, at one level, the ultimate goods for which the soul was made—and it's no surprise that we would desire the delight that accompanies the attainment of these goods.

On the other hand, I've argued that the only delights marijuana can give are misguided. They aren't healthy, normal delights, because they respond not to the goodness of reality but to the chemical effects of the drug on the brain.

Now it's time to bring these two points together. Why does marijuana use look and feel so much like genuine, wholesome delight? How do recreational drugs mimic and substitute for the ultimate goods for which we were made?

In other words, we should explicitly contrast the feelings of the weed user and those of the person who is fulfilling the demands of his humanity.

HOW TO FEEL GOOD and HOW NOT TO

Rest versus "Mellowness"

We've talked about the first and primordial celebration of the soul —namely a celebration of *being*, the existence of oneself and of the world.

Josef Pieper describes recreation, or leisure, as "an attitude of non-activity, of inward calm, of silence; it means not being 'busy,' but letting things happen."[39] He also says it is "man's happy and cheerful affirmation of his own being, his acquiescence in the world and in God."[40]

But that sounds like the attitude of a stereotypical pothead, doesn't it?

If rest is a fundamental good, a peace of the soul that flows from the acceptance of one's own being and the being of the world, then don't marijuana users tend to be pretty adept at that art? They seem to appreciate the world and themselves ("It's all good. I'm okay, you're okay"). They seem to be able to avoid being too busy and to prioritize letting things happen over getting things done ("Slow down, take it easy. Enjoy the ride"). On the surface, it might be hard to see why mellowness isn't just a form of restfulness.

Well, is that how it works with other drugs? Take alcohol. We'll talk thematically about alcohol in the next chapter, but maybe we can anticipate that discussion and use beer as an analogy for understanding why drug-induced states aren't the same as the fully human states they simulate.

So, what would we think if a man said he needed five beers in order to find a certain woman attractive? It's pretty obvious that we'd infer that the guy didn't really think the woman was attractive. His bogus attraction would be due to the chemical manipulation,

[39] *Leisure*, 46.
[40] Ibid., 65.

44

as opposed to an actual perception of her objectively attractive qualities.

By the same token, what should we think when someone smokes weed in order to appreciate reality? Again, I think in such a case we'd be justified in concluding that the person didn't actually think reality was all that great; otherwise, he wouldn't have recourse to a drug in order to feel good about existence, whether his own or the world's.

And that means smoking weed isn't leisure. It's a substitute for leisure. It's what someone does *instead of* opening himself up to being.

The propensity of the marijuana user for inactivity, then, doesn't derive from rest, because it isn't the fruit of a recognition of the goodness of things. Weed can sedate, but it can't bring peace. It can tranquilize, but it can't give tranquility.

Tranquility comes only when things are the way they're supposed to be. If things aren't right, why should we be all right with everything? And that means, if our peace is to be more than an illusion, we have to be able to (a) see the rightness of things and (b) establish that rightness within ourselves.

Contemplation versus "Feeling Insightful"

I said before that it is a profound delight to be able to reflect on the deepest issues of life, to be able to marvel at the way things are and celebrate the ultimate truths.

And here, too, it seems at first as if marijuana could help. People may have "deep" conversations when they're high. They might marvel at all kinds of quotidian things or feel as if they have core insights into themselves and into the world around them.

But, as I noted, if a thought is caused by stimulating the brain and not by conformity to reality, it's not contemplation. Cannabis, when used as a drug, impairs basic mental functions such as memory and problem-solving; it doesn't enhance them.

And yet it's a strange irony of the human condition that the uninformed and the intellectually undisciplined are often the most opinionated. Great minds tend to be humble; as the old saying goes, the more you know, the more you realize how little you know. Stupid people, on the other hand, can't think clearly enough to recognize their own intellectual limits, and instead disdain what they regard as the stupidity of everyone else.

Certainly that goes for a lot of drug-induced "thinking." Again, consider alcohol. Dave Barry's 1981 column "How to Argue Effectively" jokes that if you can't think of something intelligent to say, start drinking heavily and you'll soon feel very intelligent indeed:

> Suppose you are at a party and some hotshot intellectual is expounding on the economy of Peru, a subject you know nothing about. If you're drinking some health-fanatic drink like grapefruit juice, you'll hang back, afraid to display your ignorance, while the hotshot enthralls your date. But if you drink several large martinis, you'll discover you have *strong views* about the Peruvian economy. You'll be a *wealth* of information. You'll argue forcefully, offering searing insights and possibly upsetting furniture. People will be impressed. Some may leave the room.

The point is that the pleasure and the intellectual self-satisfaction associated with drug use come not from the mind working well but from the mind working poorly.

So once more, marijuana stimulates a feeling that misses the mark. It doesn't provide the enjoyment of contemplating truth. It provides enjoyment by hampering the contemplation of truth. It may make it easier to feel thoughtful, but it makes it harder to think.

To delight in the truth, you first have to know the truth. And that takes hard work. It takes research and rigor and a radical commitment to intellectual honesty. And smoking marijuana will provide you with exactly none of those.

Community versus "Benevolence"

We pointed out earlier that recreational drugs are often taken with other people, a fact that's sometimes used to argue that drugs promote sociability. But meaningful social interaction requires more than just shared space: it requires shared experience. And the only platform that can enable shared experience is the real world.

Reality alone can unite two minds, because reality is how each mind gets out of itself. Why can we both look at the same tree at the same time? Because the tree is in the real world. And why can we *not* both dream the same dream at the same time? Because the dream is just in our heads. So the more we stimulate mental experiences independently of the external world, the less capable we are of engaging with those around us.

More than that, the joy of love, as we said, consists in celebrating the goodness of the other—in being happy at another's happiness and rejoicing in another's fulfillment.

But of course love can't stop there. Love doesn't enjoy just hanging out or doing something fun together. Love means a willingness to serve others, to sacrifice yourself for them, to lay down your life for a friend.

Drugs don't help with that. They may make you feel good about yourself or benevolent toward others, but they don't give you good habits or make you committed to serving your neighbor self-sacrificially. Quite the opposite. Because these drugs simulate the enjoyment of social interaction independently of any charitable activity, they lead instead to an evaluation of your relationships based on the satisfaction they give you.

People who do drugs may feel suffused with an attitude of love for everyone and everything, but that doesn't make their actions any less selfish. One woman, for instance, reported having a powerful experience of love while experimenting with psychedelics and then decided to divorce her husband when he was late to pick her up later that day![41]

Let's use alcohol as an analogy once more. Christopher Hitchens, the late essayist and atheistic activist, wrote that alcohol "makes other people, and indeed life itself, a good deal less boring."[42] The obvious implication is that Hitchens didn't really think people were interesting or worthwhile in themselves—any more than the hypothetical guy mentioned earlier really thinks a woman is beautiful if he has to down a lot of drinks to feel that way.

So, if you're using drugs to make you care about other people, it's a pretty good indication that you don't really care about other people.

The takeaway is that real delights of the soul require discipline. It takes time and effort and a lot of practice to be recollected, to

---

[41] Pollan, *How to Change Your Mind*, 73. In the case of other studies, Pollan further reports that subjects "became 'much less judgmental, much less rigid, more open, and less defended.' But it wasn't all sweetness and light: several clients abruptly broke off marriages" (178). Although people often describe the experience on psychedelics as one of a humbling reconnection with all reality, the experience doesn't actually cause humility: "It is one of the many paradoxes of psychedelics that these drugs can sponsor an ego-dissolving experience that in some people quickly leads to massive ego inflation" (193).

[42] Introduction to Kingsley Amis, *Everyday Drinking: The Distilled Kingsley Amis* (New York: Bloomsbury, 2008), x.

quiet the soul, to think deeply and clearly, to understand and love those around you.

We should all be doing these things, because they will make us happy. But there's no substitute for putting in the work.

We weren't made to rest or take delight in artificially stimulated brain states. We were made to rest in human goods, in the actual flourishing of our natures. Recreational drug use—including the various forms of recreational use of cannabis—manipulates the faculties against their intended design, distracts us from the practices that facilitate virtuous delight, and makes our pursuit of real happiness that much less likely.

I've used alcohol as an illustration throughout this chapter to argue that when a recreational act of the soul is drug induced, we don't, and shouldn't, trust its genuineness. In this case, the accompanying delight is also disqualified de facto as being genuinely recreational.

But if these examples show that using cannabis as a drug can't be recreational, don't they show even more strongly that using alcohol as a drug can't be recreational?

Probably. But as we'll see in the next chapter, there may be ways to use alcohol, and use it recreationally, that don't depend on its agency as a drug at all.

6

Alcohol: Recreational Drug or Recreational Beverage?

Alcohol, as we said at the beginning, is indisputably a drug. That is to say, it's a psychoactive chemical, and one that can powerfully inhibit your intelligence and freedom. It can also have a drastic effect on your mood and is often used to achieve such an effect. If marijuana is used as a drug to make the user feel good, and antidepressants are used as drugs to stop the user from feeling bad, then alcohol is familiar for its use in both capacities.

You can use alcohol as a recreational drug, as a chemical catalyst for enjoyment. If a group goes to a bar and orders a couple of rounds of shots, "just to get the party started," it's pretty clear they're using the alcohol as a neurological switch that can flip on the feel-good setting in the brain. If it's a matter of trying to engineer delight by chemically stimulating the brain, this kind of drinking is open to the same kinds of criticism I've leveled in the preceding chapters against recreational marijuana use.

Alcohol can also be used as an emotionally therapeutic drug. You can use alcohol as a painkiller, whether physical or psychological. Old Civil War movies show field doctors using liquor as an anesthetic during operations — if whiskey was all you had during an amputation, you gave the guy as much whiskey as possible to dull the pain (yes, that might get him drunk, but the drunkenness in that case is an unintended side effect of the anesthetic). Similarly, if a man's fiancée unexpectedly breaks up with him, and he goes to a bar and asks for something, anything, "as long as it's strong," he's probably taking the drink not so he can have a good time but so he can get a handle on his emotional distress.

This latter kind of drinking is technically self-medicating, and you don't want to get into the regular habit of taking booze to deal with your problems. Samuel Johnson, who went for long periods without drinking, was once offered the following argument on behalf of alcohol: "You know, Sir, drinking drives away care, and makes us forget whatever is disagreeable. Would not you allow a man to drink for that reason?" Johnson replied, "Yes, Sir, if he sat next to *you*."[43] The point is well taken. We shouldn't need a glass of something to help us cultivate joy or get through a small unpleasantness. If Johnson's interlocutor was interesting, the pleasure in his company should make itself felt without drink, and if uninteresting, the displeasure in his company should be borne without the recourse to a drug.

That being said, if you *don't* already have a drinking problem, it seems reasonable enough to take a strong drink, or a couple of glasses of wine, in order to reduce an excessive emotional reaction in the case of an uncommon shock to the psyche. As we'll see in later chapters, there are good reasons to maintain that therapeutic drug use shouldn't be ethically off-limits.

But surely, whether it's for recreational or therapeutic purposes, in the cases considered above, alcohol is being used *as a drug*. In other words, in such cases, the person is trying to leverage the effect of alcohol on the brain in order to achieve a specific mental or emotional state.

---

[43] James Boswell, *The Life of Samuel Johnson*, ed. John Canning (London: Methuen, 1991), 138.

What I want to argue is that alcohol needn't be used as a drug at all.[44] On the contrary, the way alcohol is often used corresponds precisely to what alcohol actually is—namely, a good drink. And that use, I think, distinguishes it sharply from the use to which marijuana is typically put.

The Good of Alcohol

In the first of his pastoral epistles to Timothy, St. Paul delivers the following exhortation: "Stop drinking only water, but have a little wine for the sake of your stomach and your frequent illnesses" (1 Tim. 5:23). Our contemporary categorization of alcohol as simply a recreational beverage can make us forget that for a great deal of human history, alcoholic drinks were desired largely for their health benefits. In his historical study of alcohol, Rod Phillips argues that for long periods, when clean potable water was not easily come by, alcoholic beverages were often the safest, healthiest available drinks.[45] In Sigrid Undset's Nobel-winning *Kristin Lavransdatter*, the eponymous medieval character dutifully drinks plenty of ale during her pregnancy, for the sake of the baby's health.

Even today, many people—including some of the longest-lived—maintain the physical benefits of temperate but consistent

---

[44] The *Catechism*, in paragraph 2290, classes alcohol with food, to-bacco, and medicine, as a substance whose abuse is avoided with temperance. In the following paragraph, it discusses the use of drugs and makes the distinction between therapeutic and nontherapeutic uses (the latter being a grave moral offense). The implication seems to be that the *Catechism* considers the use of alcohol, at least in some cases, *not* to qualify as drug use.

[45] Rod Phillips, *Alcohol: A History* (Chapel Hill, NC: University of North Carolina Press, 2014), 4, 173–193.

consumption of wine or beer. Alcohol is, after all, digestible and, depending on the drink in question, offers a variety of nutrients.[46]

Alcohol even has disinfectant properties. I remember one time as a kid watching Mother Angelica on television telling the story of an Irish priest who took two worms and placed one in a glass of water and the other in a glass of whiskey. The worm in the glass of water swam around, but the worm in the glass of whiskey sank straight to the bottom. The priest looked at Mother Angelica, and said, "Do you know what lesson this teaches us?" Mother Angelica suggested perhaps that it was a sign of the deadly potential of alcohol. The priest said, "No! It means if you drink whiskey, you won't get worms!"

Granted, that's just a silly story, but it illustrates the strong, traditional view that holds that alcohol, in moderate amounts, can be beneficial for the body.

Moreover, alcoholic beverages are vehicles for delight in a finely crafted, exquisite human artifact. Delight is meant to be a response to a real good. And taking delight in something that's really excellent is a wholesome, authentically human experience. It is a true recreational activity.

Roger Scruton distinguishes the pleasurable effects of alcohol according to whether the pleasure is proper to people or common to the beasts. "Animals can be drunk; they can be high on drugs and fuggy with cannabis." By contrast, only the embodied rationality of a human being allows for the elated appreciation of a superb vintage. "Relishing is something that only a rational being can exhibit, and which therefore only a rational being can do."[47]

---

[46] "Within reasonable limits, wine is a nourishment." Pontifical Council for Pastoral Assistance, *Charter for Healthcare Workers* (January 1, 1995), no. 97.

[47] Roger Scruton, *I Drink, Therefore I Am* (London: Continuum, 2009), 126.

I myself do not have a particularly refined sense of smell or taste, so I don't go out of my way to smell or swirl my wine or whiskey or beer before drinking it, but my lack of sophistication in this particular aesthetic arena doesn't give me the right to deny that others have a greater sensibility than I do. And I can still say, and still do say, in my own philistine way, "This is really good" when I sip something excellent.

To repeat, it seems to me that this is the normal use to which alcohol is put. When I go to a friend's house, the host may ask me: "What can I get you to drink? Tea? Juice? Beer? Wine?" and he says all these things in the same tone. The mood-altering effects of alcohol don't enter into his offer or my choice. It would be bizarre for me to say, "Actually, I'm in the mood for tea, but maybe I could swallow a couple of fingers of some strong alcohol first, just so I could get a good buzz going?" My choice will be based on what would be delightful to sip, not on what will chemically manipulate my feelings. Chesterton expressed the same principle when he said, "It is quite a mistake to suppose that, when a man desires an alcoholic drink, he necessarily desires alcohol."[48]

Psalm 104 gives thanks to God for "wine that gladdens man's heart" (see v. 15). I've heard people defend drug use with this verse, as though the psalmist is celebrating the emotionally intoxicating qualities, i.e., the drug potential, of alcohol. But of course in the same verse, God is thanked for "bread that strengthens man's heart," and elsewhere in the Psalms we read that the law of the Lord "delights the heart" (see 19:8). It seems pretty clear that bread and God's law don't move or uphold the passions by some neurological mechanism: they delight and fortify because they are *good*.

---

[48] G. K. Chesterton, "Wine When It Is Red," in *All Things Considered* (New York: John Lane, 1916), 232.

So, too, does wine (or beer or whiskey) delight because it is good. It is the fruit of the vine and work of human hands. It nourishes the body, pleases the palate, warms the chest, and delights our aesthetic sensibility. When the steward tasted the wine miraculously manufactured at the wedding at Cana, he didn't comment on its strength, on its ability to stimulate the emotions. He assessed its quality and declared it to be the best.

Drink or Drug?

Now it's time to get down to the business of distinguishing recreational marijuana from the appreciative enjoyment of alcohol. And really, what basis can there be for any intrinsic moral distinction? Connoisseurship regarding cannabis is already deeply entrenched in the marijuana crowd. People take pleasure in the horticultural aspect, in the careful flavoring of the weed, and in developing cultural preferences for pairing kinds of cannabis with certain foods and drinks. So if alcoholic drinks can be celebrated as objects of beauty, why not think the same of "fine bud"?

It seems plain to me that both alcohol and marijuana could theoretically be used (a) as a recreational drug (i.e., to chemically stimulate pleasurable feelings), (b) as something for appreciative enjoyment (as an object of beauty), or (c) as both.

And yet I believe there's a profound difference in what users are actually trying to do in the two cases.

Let me give an imaginary example: suppose someone invented a handheld device with a single button on its surface. We'll call the device "the Hedonator." Pushing the button on the device is supposed to send radio signals to the brain so as to produce a general feeling of emotional delight. That's the point of the device. That's its purpose. If you pushed the button, and you didn't feel anything, you'd be disappointed, and you'd wonder why the Hedonator wasn't working.

Now suppose over time Hedonator manufacturers worked to make the device more aesthetically pleasing. Suppose they made the outside of the box out of sweet-smelling cedar and made the button out of a rich, dark rosewood. Maybe they carve lovely, intricate engravings over the whole thing. Fine—but the point of pushing that button is still to manipulate your brain state for pleasure. That's why, regardless of how ornamented the device were to become, if you pushed the button and didn't feel anything, you'd be disappointed, and you'd wonder why the Hedonator wasn't working.

I think that's a fair analogue for marijuana use: even the most culturally enriched recreational weed is still designed to give *some* high, some chemically based emotional enhancement. If all he had was the taste in his mouth and the heat in his chest—if he wasn't feeling the psychological effect—I think your typical marijuana user would wonder what was wrong (defective product? built-up resistance on the part of the user?). In other words, I think that smoking or eating cannabis is designed to function as a psychoactive drug, and I think the disappointment in the lack of felt experience is a good indicator that the user is looking precisely for that drug effect.

By contrast, alcohol isn't meant to function primarily as a drug. It hydrates and it nutrifies and it tastes good. I've never served beer or wine or whiskey and had a guest complain that they didn't know what was wrong, but they weren't feeling anything yet. If an alcoholic drink tastes good and feels good going down, people say, "This is good stuff." They affirm it as good right away; they don't have to wait and see how they feel later on. I'm sure it happens in some settings, but in my circle at least, no one ever expresses any genuine disappointment that his emotional state wasn't changing as the result of an alcoholic drink. So if we again take disappointment (or the lack thereof) as our gauge, it seems as if people aren't normally drinking with the goal of chemically altering their mood.

HOW TO FEEL GOOD and HOW NOT TO

To summarize: alcohol may chemically alter your feelings, but that's not the typical reason why people drink, whereas cannabis may provide an opportunity for aesthetic appreciation of the substance itself, but that's not the typical reason why people smoke pot.

The normal use of alcohol is geared toward nutrition, hydration, and appreciative enjoyment. Recreational use of marijuana is geared toward emotional intoxication. So it turns out that there is a fundamental distinction between the two.

Occasionally I've been asked, "Wait, but if drinkers aren't looking for the psychoactive drug effects of alcohol, why don't they just drink nonalcoholic beer or wine or whiskey?" This, to me, is like asking why we don't leave the horseradish out of cocktail sauce, or the hot sauce out of chili. It's like asking why we don't have soup cold. People, especially grown-ups, enjoy caustic foods and drinks. We like things with a kick, and we like things that warm us up. Alcohol gives drinks their burn, and it's a good burn — a heat in the mouth and throat and chest. If people prefer nonalcoholic drinks, that's perfectly fine, but those drinks lack more than just alcohol's intoxicating quality.

By the way, I'm not giving a kind of ethical carte blanche to alcohol use in any form. You can use booze to get drunk. You can use booze to create a deceptive sense of well-being.[49] You can use booze as a way of failing to deal with your problems. You can develop addiction and damage your health with booze.

---

[49] I've often heard Aquinas quoted to the effect that it's permissible to drink oneself into a state of giddiness. I don't think Aquinas ever said, "Drink to the point of hilarity" — it's one of those urban Catholic legends that gets around — but even if he did, he probably meant that once you notice yourself getting jolly from drink, it's time to stop drinking. Surely he didn't mean, and never said, that it's permissible deliberately to use wine to stimulate or simulate joy.

Most of us tend to distance ourselves from a puritan condemnation of alcohol as such, and rightly so. But that doesn't justify drinking irresponsibly or acting as though alcohol is a prerequisite to having a good time.

Alcoholic drinks are fine things, and recognizing their goodness can be a source of genuine delight. But there are many goods, many sources of delight. To anchor your enjoyment disproportionately to one kind of good, and a potentially intoxicating good at that, is to narrow the field of human happiness and open the door to chemical dependency. And, as we'll see in the next chapter, addiction to alcohol will spoil not only the alcoholic's life, but even his ability to appreciate the beautiful character of a fine drink.

7

Beauty: Uniting Delight
of Matter and Mind

Emotions, as we've said before and we'll say again, bridge the material and immaterial realms. That's why a spiritual insight can trigger a warm glow in the body, and a good drink can remind you about how wonderful the fact of existence really is.

Now it seems to me, as the preceding chapter indicates, that there's a fundamental difference between ordinary recreational marijuana use and ordinary recreational alcohol use.

In both cases the person consumes something to experience psychological delight, which is to say, in both cases, you introduce something into the body to try to achieve a state of the soul.

But in one of these cases, the person is attempting to leverage a cerebral mechanism using a physical catalyst. In the other case, the person is attempting to perceive the spiritual reality that is embedded in the object he is consuming.

How can a spiritual reality be embedded in a physical object? And why does the perception of a spiritual reality embedded in a physical object give delight?

The answer demands a consideration of the nature and experience of beauty.

HOW TO FEEL GOOD and HOW NOT TO

What Is Beauty?

There are about as many theories of beauty as there are philosophers of beauty, but I think it's possible to synthesize the different descriptions of beauty more or less by using the following formula: beauty consists in *order* and *surprise* together.

Order happens when something corresponds to its own nature, when it follows the pattern of its essence. A thing is orderly when it is what it's supposed to be and does what it's supposed to do. Order is expressed in regularity, proportion, consistency. According to Aristotle, the chief forms of beauty are "order and symmetry and definiteness."[50]

Order, things being just right, fitting together the way they're supposed to, gives a particularly soothing enjoyment. Think of how satisfying it is when you finish a jigsaw puzzle, or hear a musical chord progression resolve to the tonic, or see a clean room with everything put in its proper place. It gives a sense of peace, of delightful tranquility.

The other component of beauty is *surprise*. Surprise happens when something grabs the mind's attention by not being obvious. When something is new, unusual, marvelous, wonderful, we notice it and take delight in devoting our mental energies to it. Fulton Sheen tells us that "Beauty has two elements: one is surprise, and the other is love in the eyes of the beholder."[51] Aquinas, when discussing causes of pleasure, identifies the wonderful, unusual, and novel as genuine sources of attentive delight:

---

[50] *Metaphysics*, bk. 13.

[51] Fulton J. Sheen, *Guide to Contentment* (New York: Simon and Schuster, 1967), 23. I take it that love involved in beauty is a response to the goodness or rightness, i.e., the *order*, of the object.

Whatever is wonderful is pleasing, for instance things that
are scarce … things that are of rare occurrence can be pleasant, either as regards knowledge, from the fact that we desire
to know something about them, in so far as they are wonderful; or as regards action, from the fact that "the mind is
more inclined by desire to act intensely in things that are
new" as stated in *Ethics*.[52]

The surprise aspect is where the excitement of beauty comes
in. Order without surprise may give a reassuring sense of security and propriety, but on its own it becomes banal. Boring. The
same old thing, over and over. By contrast, newness, the splendor,
the freshness of beauty demands that we never take anything for
granted—that we perfect the art of seeing unfamiliar depths in
everything, so that we can be continually surprised. Even if you've
seen the same painting, the same person, the same mountain vista
a hundred or a thousand times, if you look carefully the 1001st
time, you'll see something you didn't see before, and you'll take
delight in the inexhaustible richness of reality.

The enjoyment of beauty, therefore, just like the other recreational delights we've talked about, requires discipline. It requires
the effort needed to maintain ever deeper levels of insight. You
must always be looking intently—otherwise, you'll just settle for
banality (order without surprise), or in desperation for some excitement, you'll turn to disorder (surprise without order).

I'm convinced that, for many people, much of contemporary life
is just bouncing back and forth between these two disconnected
halves of beauty. People go to work or school and feel as if it's a
massive trap of order without surprise: dull, joyless routine, the same
pointless regularity every day. Then they go home and indulge in

---

[52] *ST*, I-II, q. 32, a. 8, c. and ad. 3.

surprise with no order: entertain themselves with perverse images of violence, horror, or disordered sexuality. And when Monday comes around, the whole miserable thing starts over.

Better for every aspect of our lives, whether in work or leisure, to keep order and surprise together.

This formula works for how we drink as well. Alcoholic drinks, as we've said, can be drunk simply for their nutritional or health benefits. But if they're really going to be recreational, if they're going to be vehicles for beauty, then they can't become habitual or excessive.

Habit will nullify the power of beer or wine or whiskey to surprise us. We'll get used to them, and when we do, they won't bring us any significant enjoyment. We won't be startled at the goodness of what we're drinking; we'll take our drinking for granted, and then what will be the point?

Whereas drinking to excess, drinking ourselves into inanity and degradation, will potentially spoil everything. We might escape our normal, everyday lives, but the new normal of sodden imbecility will be hideous.

The travesty of alcoholism, which combines habitual drinking and excessive drinking, not only ruins our lives but even makes it impossible to appreciate this beverage for which everything else has been sacrificed. It's one of the key marks of addictions, including the addiction to drink, that the object of the addict's desire no longer gives delight; all it can offer is temporary relief from the gnawing need. Thus are the Lord's terrible words fulfilled: "Those who have not will lose even the little they have" (see Matt. 13:12).

Temperance with alcohol, as with everything else connected to beauty, is the key to enjoying it and ensuring not only that it respects the body but also that it edifies the soul.

Beauty and the Senses

One of the most orderly and surprising things in existence is us. Humans are fascinating to other humans, and for good reason. What is this thing that combines angel and beast, a mind expressed through a mouth, an immortal will that shapes the world through just these hands and just these feet? An embodied spirit, the invisible lived through the visible, is a strange and lovely thing.

This is why it makes sense that we would delight in other orderly and surprising mergers of the material and immaterial. In other words, we find beauty whenever truth or goodness takes physical form.[53] It's a fine thing to know the definition of a hero, or to recognize that heroism is a demand of the moral life. But nothing compares to a story of heroism, to the concrete image of a man or a woman who gives up great goods for the sake of a greater good. For instance, I think I *know* what it means to be a good father, and I *want* to be a good father, but when recently I heard the true story of a father who drowned in a septic tank while he saved his son's life by holding him up out of the filth, I was blown away.

Or, to take another example: Christian parents *know* they're supposed to trust God with their kids, and they probably *want* to trust God with their kids, but the following concrete image will actually *move* them in response to the beauty of trust in divine providence:

> Do you remember, my sweet, absent son,
> How in the soft June days forever done
> You loved the heavens so warm and clear and high
> And when, I lifted you, soft came your cry —

---

[53] For a further discussion of the relation between beauty and the realm of the senses, see John-Mark L. Miravalle, *Beauty: What It Is and Why It Matters* (Manchester, NH: Sophia Institute Press, 2019).

HOW TO FEEL GOOD and HOW NOT TO

"Put me 'way up — 'way, 'way up, in the blue sky"?
I laughed, and said I could not, — set you down
Your gray eyes wonder-filled beneath that crown
Of bright hair gladdening me as you raced by.
Another Father now, more strong than I,
Has borne you voiceless to your dear blue sky.[54]

Again, it's the *astonishing rightness* (i.e., the surprising order) of the father's attitude in this concrete circumstance that makes such a brief poem almost unbearably beautiful.

This is precisely what the arts are designed to do: to incarnate order and surprise in something sensible or imaginable. Then we get delight in truth and in goodness, a delight in which our body shares, whether through a rush of the blood or a tingling of the skin. The *Catechism of the Catholic Church* states that "art is a form of practical wisdom uniting knowledge and skill (cf. Wisd. 7:16–17), to give form to the truth of reality in a language accessible to sight or hearing" (2501).

I've said that beauty comes to us through the senses. In beauty, we rest not just in a concept, or in a good resolution, but in an *image*. It's precisely when we visualize or listen to a profound reality embodied in some physical form that we take pleasure in body and soul. Hence Aquinas's famous description of beauty as "that which *delights* when *seen*."[55]

Beauty in Touch and Taste and Smell

As the foregoing analysis suggests, beauty is traditionally most associated with the senses of sight and hearing. Even literary arts,

---

[54] George Parsons Lathrop, "The Child's Wish Granted."
[55] *ST*, I, q. 5, a. 4, ad. 1, italics mine.

such as poetry, produce a visual and, to some extent, auditory image in the mind.

The primary reason for this emphasis on sight and sound is pretty straightforward: we can appreciate beautiful sights and beautiful sounds more "spiritually," i.e., without connecting the enjoyment to any physical benefit or impulse. When I look at a beautiful painting, or when I listen to a concerto, the delight I experience is unconnected to the needs or satisfactions of the body. My delight may be concentrated on the sense datum, but it's a delight of the soul.

That being said, I think it's also important not to forget the way we instinctively ornament our bodily activities. An obvious illustration is the way table etiquette gives a ceremonial form to the body's nutrition. Not long ago, my kids asked why they needed to observe their manners at dinner, and I said "So that even when you're doing what animals do, you're not doing it like an animal."

The beasts pursue things such as copulation and warmth and food and drink, and so do we, but we don't pursue these things the same way. Our notions of sexual desirability are tied to our notions of beauty. That's not the case with elephants. Their males don't consider whether potential mates approximate the ideal of feminine form. We design our shelters according to an endless variation of architectural styles. Birds don't. They don't make Byzantine or Baroque or Spanish Colonial nests. As Chesterton says, "The very fact that a bird can get as far as building a nest, and cannot get any farther, proves that he has not a mind as man has a mind; it proves it more completely than if he built nothing at all."[56] The animals have their distinctive ways of dealing with changes in temperature, but none of them make clothes, none of them develop canons of

---

[56] G. K. Chesterton, *The Everlasting Man* (New York: Dodd, Mead, 1943), 21.

modesty, and none of them worry about whether they look seemly in what they're wearing.

We spiritualize even the needs of the body. And God Himself, on the Catholic view, has supernaturalized and sacramentalized the needs of the body beyond our wildest expectations. Sexual intercourse is not only a source of personal intimacy and the reproduction of the species; it has become an icon of God's love for humanity and Christ's love for the Church, and the vehicle for adding to the membership of the divine family. Food and drink, not to be outdone, have become the means of receiving the Body and Blood of the Lord. The source and summit of the Christian life is now something to be eaten and sipped from a cup.

So it seems we shouldn't leave touch and smell and taste out of our discussions of beauty. They, too, have been privileged to connect us to the immaterial through matter. They can give a spiritual delight through a physical good.

Delight in texture and taste and smell all come together in the production and appreciation of food and drink. Making good food and fine drink takes a lot of work. It demands a knowledge of what kinds of ingredients go well together (order), as well as a great deal of creativity (surprise). The varieties of food and drink are as diversified as any of the other timeless projects by which cultures express themselves. Those responsible for food preparation, those who work tirelessly to make the food good — that is, to make it delightful by its excellence — are consequently providing a distinctively spiritual service for their communities. They're true artists, and society needs them.

Moreover, the beauty of good food and drink requires a certain training in virtue and appreciation on the part of the recipient. Overindulgence blunts sensitivity to beauty in every area, and gluttons and drunkards lose their appreciation for good food and drink the way someone staring too long at the sun becomes blinded. And just as with other aesthetic sensibilities, immature palates need to be educated in order to appreciate refined dishes. If you leave people to their childish preferences, they'll never get beyond fast food and soda. Many people are missing out on some of the higher pleasures of eating and drinking, because they were never taught how to be open to new kinds of food or how to delight in things they should be eating (such as vegetables and other nonprocessed food).

Beauty and Alcoholic Drinks

This discussion of beauty—of spiritual reality conveyed in sensibly accessible packages—shows why alcoholic drinks can and should be vehicles for beauty. They have the potential to be good for the soul in addition to being good for the body.

Think of the creativity and craft invested in all the different wines in all the different vineyards of the world.

Consider the precise refinement of the palate necessary to become a sommelier, a wine steward, and the competitions at which these judges display their hard-earned discernment. As C. S. Lewis points out, such an ability to appreciate wine cannot be categorically divided from the ability to appreciate music: "The experiences of the expert in claret already contain elements of concentration, judgment, and disciplined perceptiveness, which are not sensual; those of the musician still contain elements which are."[57]

Not everyone will cultivate a sensitivity to the most rarefied distinctions between various kinds of wine or beer or spirits, just as not everyone will cultivate a sensitivity to the rarefied distinctions between various kinds of English poetry. But it would betray a poor

---

[57] C. S. Lewis, *The Four Loves* (New York: Harcourt, 1991), 15.

understanding if all English poetry were dismissed as incoherent rambling (even if that does describe some poems), and it would be a deep depreciation of the possibilities of wine or whiskey or spirits if they were all dismissed as just being a drug.

Part 3

Drugs Taken to Reduce Sorrow

8

Depression and Prescription Drugs

It's time to transition from the topic of substances consumed for pleasure to that of substances consumed in order to alleviate distress. Although marijuana and alcohol could certainly be resorted to by someone going through an emotional crisis, such uses are generally regarded as exceptional. Antidepressants, on the other hand, are increasingly seen as a standard medical treatment for those suffering from prolonged and generalized unhappiness.

There's really no way to talk about antidepressants except within the context of depression, not only because that's what the drugs are for, but also because, as we'll see, contemporary ideas about antidepressants and contemporary ideas about depression have developed in such a way that each set of ideas relies on the other. This means that we had better have a clear sense of what depression is if we want to get a good conceptual handle on antidepressants.

I'm going to start this chapter by saying two things that I'll restate further on, and at greater length, but I think they need to be said here so that people don't get the wrong idea. First, I don't think it's morally impermissible to take antidepressants. They can be a legitimate part of a whole-person approach to depression. Again, I'll unpack that later on. Second, I do think that there's a physiological component to depression, because there's a physiological component to basically *every* human experience, especially, as we've seen, where the emotions are involved.

What I do want to argue, though, is that depression is not *just* a body thing. I don't think any aspect of our lives, especially our psychic lives, should be reduced to just the physical level. My goal in this chapter is not to be "unscientific," or to discount the findings of neuroscientists—quite the contrary: I wish more people were aware of exactly what science does and does not tell us about depression—but to challenge the idea that our character and our emotions are nothing more than the results of neurochemical reactions firing around in our skull.

And by the way, that doesn't mean that being depressed is the depressed person's fault, or that depressed patients just need to snap out of it. No one is saying that. I'm certainly not. All I want to suggest is that we have to appreciate the full human reality of depression if our response is going to be proportionate to the needs of both our bodies and our souls.

Okay, with those disclaimers out of the way, let's look at the nature of depression.

"Burdening the Soul"

When suffering is intense, and especially when it's long-lasting, we instinctively describe the experience through metaphors of weight. We feel as if we have heavy boots, we're crushed, we're weighed down. We're depressed.

For Aquinas, depression[58] is one of the primary effects of sorrow. In such cases, suffering causes the person to turn inward and focus on the pain itself, distracting the person from any other fact. Sometimes the sorrow of the depressed person still allows for and

---

[58] He uses *aggravare* from *ad* (to) and *gravare* (weigh down).

even motivates action that can help the situation. But sometimes the anguish is so severe that the person becomes psychologically, and sometimes even physically, immobilized:

> If, on the other hand, the strength of the evil be such as to exclude the hope of evasion, then even the interior movement of the afflicted soul is absolutely hindered, so that it cannot turn aside either this way or that. Sometimes even the external movement of the body is paralyzed, so that a man becomes completely stupefied.[59]

So we're looking at a situation in which "the soul, through being depressed so as to be unable to attend freely to outward things, withdraws to itself, closing itself up as it were."[60] This is clearly a concerning situation since it runs the risk of cutting the person off from reality, sealed in a morbid enclosure, alone with the hurt. Fortunately, Aquinas has multiple remedies to suggest, but before getting to the solution we need to spend some more time understanding the problem.

Aquinas's analysis of depression fits pretty well with the contemporary use of the word "depression" as a prolonged state of unhappiness that makes it hard to acknowledge and appreciate anything else. But where does this state come from?

Suffering, like the other emotions, can originate in the body or the mind. It can be in response to a physical ailment or to a spiritual trial. Long physical illnesses can wipe people out, make it hard for them to think about anything other than their pain or debilitation. St. John Henry Newman writes:

> Many persons have an anxious self-tormenting disposition, or depression of spirits, or deadness of the affections, in

---

[59] *ST*, I-II, q. 37, a. 2.
[60] Ibid., ad. 2.

consequence of continued or peculiar ill-health; and though it is their study, as it is their duty, to strive against this evil as much as they can, yet it often may be impossible to be rid of it.[61]

Long or intense suffering, or both, in response to spiritual crises can also consume the soul. When St. Bernard's brother died, he made an effort to carry on, to keep steady and consistent in his regular habits and duties. Then one day, in the middle of a series of sermons on the Song of Songs, he interrupted his meditation, saying, "I, whose life is bitterness, what have I to do with this canticle? Overpowering sorrow distracts my mind, the displeasure of the Lord drains my spirit dry.... The sorrow that I suppressed struck deeper roots within, growing all the more bitter, I realized, because it found no outlet."[62]

Or take depression as a response to brutal moral evil. In Tom Wolfe's *I Am Charlotte Simmons*, the eponymous character is sent into a spiraling depression after being sexually manipulated and then humiliated by a degenerate frat boy. She goes from a bright, confident, academically promising student to nearly failing out of school since she can't focus enough even to leave her room and get to class.

These kinds of depression are easy to understand: something bad has happened, and the soul is so locked on the badness that nothing else seems to matter.

Lately, however, especially in the last fifty years or so, depression has been recast by many people not as a response to physical pain or a response to psychological suffering, but instead as a *defect in our*

---

[61] St. John Henry Newman, "The State of Grace," in *Parochial and Plain Sermons* (San Francisco: Ignatius Press, 1997), 818–819.
[62] Bernard of Clairvaux, *Sermons on the Song of Songs*, XXVI.

cerebral apparatus. In other words, they think depression happens because something has gone wrong with our brains.[63]

Admittedly, there's some initial plausibility to this view since we know that brain dysfunctions can cause emotional disorders. Phineas P. Gage had an iron rod accidentally driven through his brain. He survived but was emotionally unstable for the rest of his life.[64] Heavy narcotics disrupt emotions by disrupting the brain, and even going a long time without sleep can make a person vacillate between giddiness and deep dejection.

So is depression just an indication that something's wrong with your brain?

Looking for a Biological Correlate to Depression

Scientists have been looking for a physiological marker for depression for decades. But after all this time, after all the money and the research, they haven't found one. The current *Diagnostic and Statistical Manual of Mental Disorders*, also known as the *DSM-5*, admits that "no laboratory test has yielded results of sufficient

---

[63] See Joanna Moncrieff: "The chemical imbalance has since become the ubiquitous justification for mind-altering substances. Despite the fact that it has long been accepted as false, or at least unproven, the idea continues to be cited as the basis for the action of drugs in depression.... The message has been so successfully diffused throughout society that most members of the general public have been convinced that chemical abnormalities have been established in depression and that these abnormalities are corrected by antidepressants." "Opium and the People: The Prescription Psychopharmaceutical Epidemic in Historical Context" in *The Sedated Society*, ed. James Davies (Cham, Switzerland: Palgrave Macmillan, 2017), 73–99, 92.

[64] See Nancey Murphy, *Bodies and Souls, or Spirited Bodies?* (New York: Cambridge University Press, 2006), 67.

sensitivity and specificity to be used as a diagnostic tool for this disorder."[65] In other words, they can't physically test for depression. They can't check your brain, they can't check your chemicals, and say, "We just got the lab results back. It's what we thought: you're positive for depression."

To put it very clearly: scientists and psychologists can't find anything distinctively wrong, or even anything distinctively *different*, with the brains and bodies of depressed people. Although an enormous number of people are being diagnosed with depression, "such diagnostic inflation did not emerge from any advance in biological research (there are still no discovered bio-markers for nearly all mental disorders)."[66]

Sometimes you'll hear people stressing the difference between "regular" depression and "clinical" depression, but there's no biological difference. A diagnosis of clinical depression simply means, as the word suggests, that the patient visited a professional in some kind of clinical setting, and the professional, after hearing what the patient had to say, decided that the patient met the necessary criteria to merit the label "depressed." But there was no biochemical diagnostic test during the session because there's no biochemical diagnostic test out there.

And even if they did find a biological marker, that test wouldn't give us a definitive understanding about the nature and cause of depression. Any biological marker for depression would be necessarily provisional, because one day we might find cases in which that gauge didn't work. Vladimir Maletic and Charles Raison imagine the limits of any physiological test that may be developed in the future:

---

[65] *Diagnostic and Statistical Manual of Mental Disorders*, 5th ed. (Washington, DC: American Psychiatric Association, 2013), 165.

[66] James Davies, introduction to *The Sedated Society*, 5–6.

Again, we consider two patients who present to your office, but this time they arrive in some golden future age when a biomarker for Major Depression has been identified.

The first patient breaks down sobbing when you begin inquiring into his emotional state. Upon further questioning he is found to have nine out of nine criteria for Major Depression.[67] A call to his wife confirms that these symptoms have crippled every aspect of his life. Just to be sure that he does indeed have Major Depression, you obtain a little blood and send it off for the diagnostic lab test. Remarkably, the test comes back negative. What would you do? Would you tell the patient that he does not have Major Depression because the test is negative and that therefore you can't treat him? Or would you ignore the test and commence either psycho or medicinal therapy?

In contrast to the first patient, the second patient presents to your office in a completely normal state of mind. He denies all depressive symptoms emphatically. A call to his wife confirms that the patient appears to be enjoying life fully and functioning at a near optimal level. If for no other reason than to protect yourself legally, you draw some blood and send it off for the diagnostic blood test. Amazingly, despite this patient's total lack of symptoms, his diagnostic test comes back as positive for Major Depression. Would you call him back and tell him he is sick with Major Depression but just doesn't know it? Would you start him on an antidepressant?[68]

---

[67] E.g., feelings of worthlessness, thoughts of guilt, markedly diminished interest or pleasure in all, or almost all, activities most of the day, and so forth. See *DSM-5*, 160–161.

[68] Vladimir Maletic and Charles Raison, *The New Mind-Body Science of Depression* (New York: Norton, 2017), 16–17.

HOW TO FEEL GOOD and HOW NOT TO

This thought-experiment shows that when it comes to depression, you can't take the testimony of the body against the testimony of the soul. Why not? Because as we saw in chapter 2, the power of feeling is in the soul: "the movement of pain is always in the soul."[69] It's not in the body as such. Oxygen can't feel pain, and carbon can't feel sorrow, and neither can hydrogen, nitrogen, calcium, phosphorus, potassium, sulfur, sodium, chlorine, or magnesium—and the human body is just these eleven elements in combination.

The final criterion for whether you feel depressed isn't what your body is doing, but *whether you feel depressed*. The feeling state isn't the same as the body state, so you can't comprehend the first just by looking at the second.

It's also crucial to remember that correlation doesn't prove causation: it might be that certain physiological phenomena tend to accompany psychological phenomena, but that doesn't tell you which caused which:

> Even if a biochemical imbalance were found in some depressed patients, this would not necessarily mean that it was the cause of the problem. Suppose one day you were standing on a street corner waiting for the bus home when someone came along and robbed you at gunpoint. Your assailant heaps abuse and death threats upon you as he absconds with your money, jewelry, and other valuables. You are left traumatized and panicked at the thought that he will return for you. If you ran to the nearest medical clinic, you might well be diagnosed with a biochemical imbalance. All kinds of stress hormones and chemical signals would be coursing through your brain and body. But these biochemical events would be the result of your psychological distress, not the cause.

---

[69] St. Thomas Aquinas, *ST*, I-II, q. 35, a. 1, ad. 1.

They would be the cart, not the horse.... If a biochemical imbalance is ever found, it should come as no surprise that psychological states have physiological correlates.[70]

We don't really have a good lie detector test, but if we ever get one, it won't be because things such as breathing and heart-rate patterns cause people to tell lies, but because telling lies affects our breathing and heart rate. Likewise, a biological marker for depression wouldn't tell us that depression is biochemically caused—only that it usually has physical symptoms.

To summarize:

• There's currently no known physical condition that corresponds to depression.

• Depression is a feeling, not a body state, so you couldn't logically deduce one from the presence of the other.

• Even if there was a marker that typically accompanied depression, it wouldn't indicate that the physical condition caused the depression.

The surprising truth is that science simply does not support the view that depression is a brain malfunction. "Not only is the chemical imbalance hypothesis unproven," says Irving Kirsch, "it is about as close as a theory gets in science to being disproven by the evidence."[71] In this case, how can it be that so many people are convinced that depression results from a chemical imbalance in the brain?[72]

---

[70] Joseph Glenmullen, *Prozac Backlash: Overcoming the Dangers of Prozac, Zoloft, Paxil, and Other Antidepressants with Safe, Effective Alternatives* (New York: Simon & Schuster, 2000), 198.

[71] Irving Kirsch, *The Emporer's New Drugs: Exploding the Antidepressant Myth* (New York: Basic Books, 2010), 81.

[72] Medical researcher Peter C. Gøtzsche states that "one sign that psychiatry is in crisis is that more than half the patients believe their mental disorder is caused by a chemical imbalance in the brain."

HOW TO FEEL GOOD and HOW NOT TO

Antidepressants and the Reconceiving of Depression

The simple fact of the matter is that we think about depression as a biochemical imbalance largely because antidepressant drugs came on the scene. Certain drugs were developed, depressed people reported feeling better (or less bad) on those drugs, and suddenly the idea became widespread that depression — which was now chemically treatable — is chemically caused.

Also, when pharmaceutical companies developed a drug that could be used for depressed people, they spent a great deal of energy marketing depression as a biological disease:

> Before the 1960s, clinical depression was thought to be an extremely rare problem. Drug companies stayed away from depression because there was no money to be made in antidepressants.... It is now clear to everyone that the market for antidepressants was not a shallow one at all; that it was, in fact, a tremendously lucrative market.... National Depression Awareness Day began in 1991 and is now a national media event. In October of each year, hospitals and universities around the country offer free depression screening. People are encouraged to dial twenty-four-hour 800-numbers and take an automated depression screening test.... Who pays for the press kits, the 800-numbers, and the depression screening kits? Eli Lilly, the manufacturer of Prozac.[73]

Once mental-health professionals could prescribe medication or recommend it to their patients,[74] an explanation was needed

---

Deadly Psychiatry and Organised Denial (Copenhagen: People's Press, 2015), 13.

[73] Carl Elliot, *Better Than Well: American Science Meets the American Dream* (New York: Norton, 2003), 123, 125.

[74] At present, only psychiatrists, nurse practitioners, and physician assistants can write prescriptions. Counselors, social workers, and

for (a) what the biological problem was and (b) how these medications fixed the problem. Such explanations have taken various forms, usually focusing on neurotransmitters in the synapse (although which neurotransmitters are affected, and how, was never fully agreed upon). But it didn't matter so much *what* the physical problem was; what mattered was the growing conviction that the problem *was* physical:

> Far, then, from providing answers to the questions of how antidepressants work or to the question of what is actually wrong in the nervous systems of people who are depressed, the biological investigations involved have played a different role. In essence, they have provided biological justification for the new approaches that were taken up by psychiatry during the 1970s and 1980s. They have provided artistic verisimilitude by allowing psychiatrists, who talked about biology, to appear scientific.[75]

Depressed patients are often told that their problem has something to do with neurotransmitters. As we've seen already, there is, in fact, no indication that neurotransmitter levels (serotonin, norepinephrine, dopamine, and so forth) are out of balance in depressed people:

> In reality, science does not have the ability to measure the levels of any biochemical in the tiny spaces between nerve cells (the synapses) in the brain of a human being. All the talk about biochemical imbalances is sheer speculation.[76]

psychologists can refer patients but can't prescribe.

[75] David Healy, *The Antidepressant Era* (Cambridge, MA: Harvard University Press, 1997), 164.

[76] Peter Breggin, *The Antidepressant Fact Book: What Your Doctor Won't Tell You about Prozac, Zoloft, Paxil, Celexa, and Luvox* (Cambridge, MA: Da Capo Press, 2001), 21.

HOW TO FEEL GOOD and HOW NOT TO

Granted, even if there's no indication of something, that doesn't prove the nonexistence of the thing in question. I think it was Bertrand Russell who gave the example of an invisible teapot orbiting Earth in outer space. It's true we can't prove there's no such teapot. But since there isn't any indication that such a teapot exists, we also shouldn't postulate its existence in the absence of any good reason to think it's there. And we shouldn't postulate the existence of physical diseases, or even abnormalities, unless we have a good reason to think such diseases or abnormalities exist.

Nor is it always exactly clear how the drug's action on the brain produces the desired effect of alleviating feelings of depression:

> Whereas we once spoke of drugs blocking neurotransmitter uptake, causing neurotransmitter release or depletion, or influencing receptors, today we understand that all these basic neuronal processes are, in reality, complex molecular events that involve multiple control factors. Identifying a specific molecular mechanism in a drug's action on neuronal function is, in fact, very much like a search for a needle in a haystack.... As our understanding of basic neuronal and synaptic processes increases, so does the number of potential sites or mechanisms for the expression of depressive behavior and for drug actions. The needle is still only a needle, but the haystack continues to grow larger.[77]

Of course, not knowing *how* the drugs work doesn't falsify the claim *that* they work. But unless we can identify a physical

[77] W. D. Horst, "Biochemical and Physiological Processes in Brain Function and Drug Actions" in *Antidepressants: Past, Present, and Future* (Berlin: Springer-Verlag, 2004), 4. Cf. Maletic and Raison: "All the early conceptions of how these antidepressants worked (e.g., by simply increasing serotonin or norepinephrine) have been largely discredited." *New Mind-Body Science*, 174.

disease—and what exactly the drugs do to heal that disease—we can't presume the existence either of the disease itself or of the drugs' curative agency. We keep coming back, then, to the same question: why do so many still cling to the conviction that depression is based in brain chemistry? Again, somehow the idea that *because* depression can be managed chemically, *therefore* depression must originate chemically grabbed hold of the general population. This is really bad circular reasoning. It's practically the same fallacy as saying that *because* a broken leg can be managed with crutches, *therefore* a broken leg is caused by not having crutches. By the same token, if you confuse alleviating symptoms with healing an illness, you'll be forced to conclude that handkerchiefs are the medical cure for the common cold!

That's why, when it comes to depression, it doesn't work to say, "Well, it makes depressed people feel better, so it must be fixing the original problem that caused the depression." Look at electroconvulsive therapy, which is "the application of electricity to the body in order to induce seizures, and ultimately relieve symptoms of major mental illnesses, such as severe and chronic depression."[78] You might have thought that shocking people until they have seizures as therapy for depression would be a practice of the distant past, but it's been making a comeback for nearly three decades now.[79] In fact, it's used in America on an estimated one hundred thousand people a year—again, with depression as a primary target.[80] Nobody has any definite idea as to how blasting electricity through the brain could possibly make the brain healthier, but people do it, in large numbers, because they're in such mental distress.

[78] Jonathan Sadowsky, *Electroconvulsive Therapy in America: The Anatomy of a Medical Controversy* (New York: Routledge, 2017), 2.
[79] Ibid.
[80] Mental Health America, "Electroconvulsive Therapy (ECT)," Mental Health America, www.mentalhealthamerica.net/ect.

HOW TO FEEL GOOD and HOW NOT TO

And, naturally, that mental distress has a cause, but due to the fixation on the speculated physiological causes of depression, what runs the risk of being ignored are the full human causes of depression. An obvious example is the case of postpartum depression. People focus on the hormonal changes in the woman at childbirth and may forget that having a new baby involves massive physical pain and enormous mental and emotional challenges. The disproportionate emphasis can lead to a dismissal of postpartum depression as a "chemical thing":

> While there may be a biological element to post-natal depression, this possibility has not been proven and remains purely speculative. But the emotional upheaval associated with childbirth is not speculative; it is a fact of life.... Postnatal depression is not a "mental illness." It is an understandable human response to one of the most challenging human experiences of all—becoming a mother.[81]

Depression shouldn't just be shrugged off as a kind of senseless short in the cerebral circuit. If there's no sign of a problem originating in the body, depression alerts us to the presence of a deeper problem, a problem our sorrow is urging us to find and address.

In fact, as we'll see in the next chapter, that's exactly why we have sorrow in the first place.

---

[81] Terry Lynch, *Beyond Prozac: Healing Mental Suffering without Drugs* (Dublin: Marino Books, 2001), 115.

9

The Value of Suffering

It's easy to feel as if depression is just a stupid, senseless funk — especially if you're depressed yourself. When you're depressed, there just doesn't seem to be any point to *anything*, least of all this useless, unhappy torpor you find yourself stuck in.

Of course depression, like all suffering, is unpleasant — by definition.[82] But even if it feels senseless or pointless, that doesn't mean it actually is.

And supposing there *is* some significance, some power and purpose, to suffering in general — and depression in particular — the task wouldn't be simply to attack suffering but rather to tap into its message and motive force.

Viktor Frankl, a Jewish psychiatrist and concentration-camp survivor, was committed to the idea that all suffering, including depression, had to be understood as a deeply meaningful part of human experience:

> A man's concern, even his despair, over the worthwhileness of life is an *existential distress* but by no means a *mental*

---

[82] Again, even though these words have different connotations — and, in certain contexts, different definitions — I'll use the words "sorrow," "sadness," "suffering," and "displeasure" interchangeably. If I want to specify physical hurt, I'll usually use "pain" or "physical pain."

disease. It may well be that interpreting the first in terms of the latter motivates a doctor to bury his patient's existential despair under a heap of tranquilizing drugs. It is his task, rather, to pilot the patient through his existential crises of growth and development.[83]

Consequently, before talking about what steps should be taken in response to depression, we should spend some time investigating the nature of suffering and why we have it. Without such a reflection, we may instinctively react to suffering by trying to get rid of it by whatever means necessary. And that might constitute a tragically wasted opportunity.

What Suffering Is

We'll begin our discussion of suffering by defining the word "evil." If, as Christians believe, all existence comes from God, and God is all-good, it follows that evil cannot come from God or be a form of existence. Evil, consequently, is a specific form of non-existence. It's a privation — that is, the absence of a good that should be present.

If something is bad, it's because it's missing something it should have. It's bad to be blind because it means you don't have sight; it's bad to have cancer because the cancer cells lack the proper harmony with the rest of the body in their process of replicating; and it's bad to do poorly on a test because it means that your test suffers from an absence of the right answers. Finally, it's bad, morally bad this time, to be wicked, because it means you lack the virtue — the honesty and prudence and love — you ought to have.

---

[83] Viktor Frankl, *Man's Search for Meaning: An Introduction to Logotherapy* (New York: Simon & Schuster, 1984), 108.

Now *suffering* is the *felt response to something perceived as being evil*. Within the broader category of suffering, it's helpful to distinguish between physical pain, which begins in the body, and spiritual sorrow, which begins in the rational soul.[84] Both species of suffering are unpleasant in different ways, and the crucial point is that they should be unpleasant. We ought to be repulsed by evil. We should be disgusted at the thought of eating rat poison, and we should be disgusted at the thought of an infected abscess on our skin, and we should be disgusted at the thought of torturing children for pleasure. It's not enough just to know abstractly that these things are bad; it's a sign of human excellence to feel a concrete emotional repugnance toward them:

> It is a sign of goodness if a man is in sorrow or pain on account of this present evil. For if he were not to be in sorrow or pain, this could only be either because he feels it not, or because he does not reckon it as something unbecoming, both of which are manifest evils. Consequently it is a condition of goodness, that, supposing an evil to be present, sorrow or pain should ensue.[85]

Indifference, callousness, nonchalance in the face of evil—these aren't strengths, but defects of character. We ought to dislike evil, but if we dislike evil, then when we experience evil, we will suffer.[86] And that's as it should be.

---

[84] See *ST*, I-II, q. 35, a. 2. For a discussion on Aquinas's distinction between pain and sorrow, see Robert Miner, *Thomas Aquinas on the Passions* (Cambridge: Cambridge University Press, 2009), 191–196.

[85] Aquinas, *ST*, I-II, q. 39, a. 1.

[86] Experiencing evil is equivalent to experiencing the lack or loss of a good, but we usually present evil to ourselves as something positive. E.g., we know death is just the loss of life, but we may picture

HOW TO FEEL GOOD and HOW NOT TO

People frequently confuse suffering and evil, probably because suffering always indicates the presence of some evil. If we suffer, it's either because we accurately perceive some present evil or because we mistakenly think something's evil when it isn't — and that very mistake on our part is itself a privation in our judgment.[87] So suffering doesn't happen without evil.

But the correspondence between evil and suffering shouldn't lead to an erroneous conflation. Only evil is evil. Suffering, as we've just seen, can be good. It can be the right response to a perceived evil, the sign and substance of a healthy emotional life. More than that, it can motivate change, and so improve both our understanding of things and how we live our lives. Let's look at some of the ways that can happen.

The Benefits of Suffering for the Individual

Physical pain is an easy place to begin, since it's clearly advantageous for the organism to feel repugnance for unhealthy things. Pain motivates people not to harm themselves, not to stick their hands in the fire or poke forks into their eyes. People who can't feel physical pain tend to hurt themselves much more regularly, even if they're cognitively aware that their activities are objectively damaging their bodies.[88]

Unfortunately, physical pleasure just wouldn't be enough to keep folks out of trouble. Michael J. Murray considers what would happen if, instead of feeling pain when we did something

---

and personify it as the Grim Reaper. See St. Thomas Aquinas, *ST*, I-II, q. 36, a. 1.

[87] See *ST*, I-II, q. 39, a. 4.

[88] See Philip Yancey and Paul Brand, *The Gift of Pain* (Grand Rapids, MI: Zondervan, 1997), 194–196.

unhealthy, we just felt pleasure when we stopped doing something unhealthy:

> Would such a mechanism work? It hardly seems so. To see why not, imagine the prospect of having children rewired with such an injury-avoidance mechanism. If they were to experience powerful feelings of pleasure when removing their hands from fires, one would expect them not to avoid injury, but rather to spend their afternoons sticking their hands in fires and removing them! Not exactly adaptive behavior.[89]

So pain is a basic functional response system for which there is no substitute. And the same goes for sorrow.

Sorrow, for instance, can cause us to reconsider what we think about everything. Where do you think it all comes from, and what do you think it all means? Do you think you came from nothing, and that you'll just dissipate back into nothingness a few years from now? The sorrow provoked by that vacuous outlook might prompt a more careful assessment. If you don't know what the meaning of life is, and you're unhappy about that, good — *you ought to be!*

Sorrow can also motivate moral reform. If you find yourself deprived of some good, your spiritual dissatisfaction may make you reflect on how you've either neglected that good, or, worse, discouraged that good by directly acting against it. Loneliness, for instance, might make you realize that you haven't put enough effort into relationships with friends and family, or that your habits of greed and envy and lust and anger are consistently cutting you off from other people.

---

[89] Michael J. Murray, *Nature Red in Tooth and Claw: Theism and the Problem of Animal Suffering* (Oxford: Oxford University Press, 2008), 120.

HOW TO FEEL GOOD and HOW NOT TO

Paradoxically, sorrow can even enhance our faculty for joy. Aquinas affirms that sorrow causes joy "because sadness, as actually existing, causes pleasure, inasmuch as it brings to mind that which is loved"; and moreover, "the recollection of sadness becomes a cause of pleasure."[90] In his brilliant play *The Sunset Limited*, Cormac McCarthy makes the same point in the following bit of dialogue between an uneducated black Christian and a white atheistic university professor:

> WHITE. We were born in such a fix as this. Suffering and human destiny are the same thing. Each is a description of the other.
>
> BLACK. We aint talkin about sufferin. We talkin about bein happy.
>
> WHITE. Well you can't be happy if you're in pain.
>
> BLACK. Why not?
>
> WHITE. You're not making any sense.
>
> BLACK. [*Falls back clutching his chest.*] Oh them is some hard words from the professor. The preacher has fell back. He's clutchin his heart. Eyes is rolled back in his head. Wait a minute. Wait a minute folks. His eyes is blinkin. I think he's comin back. I think he's comin back. [*Sits up and leans forward.*] The point, Professor, is that if you didnt have no pain in your life then how would you even know you *was* happy? As compared to what?[91]

Contrast is the condition for clarity in human thought and sharpness in human feeling. In this life, anyway, those who haven't suffered deeply don't have the dark background needed

<hr />

[90] *ST,* I-II, q. 32, a. 4.

[91] Cormac McCarthy, *The Sunset Limited* (New York: Vintage, 2006), 55.

to appreciate the full, incandescent splendor of the happiness they've been given.

Leading Us to God

The purpose of suffering, like the purpose of every human thing, can be fully appreciated only within the overall framework of the purpose of the whole human being. From the Christian perspective, the ultimate purpose of the human being, the ultimate goal, is union with God. Suffering can be, is meant to be, a spur that drives us forward toward the divine destination, and it plays a crucial role at every stage of that journey.

To begin with, suffering wakes the soul from spiritual sluggishness and demands that we take the question of our own existence seriously:

> We can rest contentedly in our sins and in our stupidities; and anyone who has watched gluttons shoveling down the most exquisite foods as if they did not know what they were eating, will admit that we can ignore even pleasure. But pain insists upon being attended to. God whispers to us in our pleasures, speaks in our conscience, but shouts in our pain: it is His megaphone to rouse a deaf world.[92]

Suffering will not let us rest content, because it is itself discontentment. It demands that we seek an answer, a solution to the human question. Before we even begin our journey to God, suffering motivates us to search for a path to a better mode of being.

Once we've found the path—the one road to God, the one way, the one Mediator, Jesus Christ—suffering may prevent us from

---

[92] C. S. Lewis, *The Problem of Pain* (New York: HarperCollins, 2001), 90–91.

idling, from procrastinating, from holding back too long. Augustine knew he was supposed to be a Christian, but he simply couldn't motivate himself to take the plunge into the Church and give up his old way of life. Then suddenly he sees the alternative clearly, he sees the truth about Christ and His Church and his own base character, and the pain forces him to a decision:

> I suffered from a madness that was to bring health, and I was in a death agony that was to bring life: for I knew what a thing of evil I was, but I did not know the good that I would be after but a little while.... In the shifting tides of my indecision, I made many bodily movements.... If I tore my hair, and beat my forehead, if I locked my fingers together and clasped my knees, I did so because I willed it.... Thus I was sick and tormented, and I upbraided myself much more bitterly than ever before.... Within the hidden depths of my soul, O Lord, you urged me on. By an austere mercy you redoubled the scourges of fear and shame, lest I give in again.[93]

God would not leave Augustine comfortably uncommitted. We were made to commit, and commit to Him, and anything less is unsatisfying, unpleasant—painful. And even after we make the decision to follow Christ, the temptation to mediocrity resurfaces, the temptation to treat God as an insurance policy while focusing our energies and hopes for peace of soul on this world. Again, pain prevents that deadly program from succeeding:

> Now God, who has made us, knows what we are and that our happiness lies in Him. Yet we will not seek it in Him

---

[93] *The Confessions of Saint Augustine*, bk. 8, chaps. 8, 11, trans. John K. Ryan (New York: Image, 1960), 195–196, 199–200.

as long as He leaves us any other resort where it can even plausibly be looked for. While what we call "our own life" remains agreeable we will not surrender it to Him. What then can God do in our interests but make "our own life" less agreeable to us, and take away the plausible source of false happiness?[94]

If a person hadn't eaten for a long time and was hungry, there'd be no mystery to it. By the same token, there's no mystery as to why people are dissatisfied with life. They're dissatisfied because they were made for Heaven, and they don't have Heaven. That dissatisfaction, that suffering, is precisely suited to our condition.

More than that, getting into Heaven requires perfection, since "nothing unclean" shall enter it (Rev. 21:27). But perfection means letting go, being purged, of every evil that our disordered wills and passions have come to rest in. Addiction to a toxic substance means finding pleasure in something unhealthy, or at least pain in its absence. But the addiction can be broken only as these false goods are taken away — with profound suffering as the result.

Hence the familiar theme in the spiritual tradition of the "Dark Night of the Soul," wherein God's favored holy ones are ruthlessly purified of any worldly attachment to self-satisfaction. Some classic examples:

> *St. Teresa of Avila*: I know of a person who had ceased wishing she might die so as to see God, but was desiring death in order that she might not suffer such constant distress at the thought of her ingratitude to One to Whom her debts were so great. She thought nobody's evil deeds could equal hers,

---

[94] Lewis, *The Problem of Pain*, 94.

for she believed there was no one with whom God had borne for so long and to whom He had shown so many favors.[95]

St. John of the Cross: And when the soul suffers the direct assault of this Divine light, its pain, which results from its impurity, is immense; because, when this pure light assails the soul, in order to expel its impurity, the soul feels itself to be so impure and miserable that it believes God to be against it, and thinks that it has set itself up against God. This causes it sore grief and pain, because it now believes that God has cast it away.... This is especially so at certain times when it is assailed with somewhat greater force; for sense and spirit, as if beneath some immense and dark load, are in such great pain and agony that the soul would find advantage and relief in death.[96]

St. Thérèse of Lisieux: My torment redoubles; it seems to me that the darkness, borrowing the voice of sinners, says mockingly to me: "You are dreaming about the light.... Advance, advance; rejoice in death which will give you not what you hope for but a night still more profound, the night of nothingness."[97]

St. Teresa of Calcutta: Lord, my God, who am I that You should forsake me? The child of your love—and now become as the most hated one—the one You have thrown away as

---

[95] St. Teresa of Avila, *Interior Castle*, Sixth Mansion, chap. 7, trans. E. Allison Peers (New York: Image, 1989), 170–171.

[96] St. John of the Cross, *Dark Night of the Soul*, bk. 2, chap. 5, trans. E. Allison Peers (Radford, VA: Wilder, 2008), 65.

[97] St. Thérèse of Lisieux, *Story of a Soul*, 3rd ed., chap. 10, trans. John Clarke, O.C.D. (Washington, DC: ICS Publications, 1996), 213.

unwanted—unloved.... It pains without ceasing.—I have no faith.—I dare not utter the words & thoughts that crowd in my heart—& make me suffer untold agony.... The whole time smiling—Sisters & people pass such remarks.—They think my faith, trust & love are filling my very being & that the intimacy with God and union to His will must be absorbing my heart.—Could they but know—and how my cheerfulness is the cloak by which I cover the emptiness & misery.[98]

The Church canonizes saints largely to give us models for how to live, how to be human. If the saints suffer such sorrow, even at the pinnacles of moral and spiritual excellence, it should make us hesitant to treat prolonged, profound suffering as an evil to be rid of no matter what.

Suffering itself is not an evil. Again, evil is evil. Evil is the problem. Evil—whether physical, psychological, or spiritual—is the thing to eliminate. Salvation from evil is the central moral objective.

Salvation from suffering is *not* the central moral objective. If it were, we could just organize a concerted drop of nukes on as many human habitations as possible—we'd all die instantly and painlessly, and no one would ever suffer again.

Classical theodicies present God as *allowing* evil out of respect for created freedom and interdependence, and because He can use evil as an opportunity for good. But God *gives* us the gift of human suffering for the perfection of our nature and as a motive for heroically moving beyond the weaknesses and defects of our condition: "the more one sorrows on account of a certain thing,

---

[98] Mother Teresa, *Come Be My Light: The Private Writings of the Saint of Calcutta*, ed. Brian Kolodiejchuk, M.C. (New York: Doubleday, 2007), 186–187.

the more one strives to shake off sorrow, provided there is a hope of shaking it off."[99] The story of Job tells us to avoid jumping to conclusions about exactly *what* God is working to achieve in a particular case of suffering (whether our own or someone else's), but we know it is one of His preferred means of drawing souls closer to their fulfillment.

Suffering, however, just like any other good or any other passion, can also become disordered. It can become counterproductive. It can inhibit, instead of inciting, the process of making things better. Such is the case with "excessive sorrow, which consumes the soul: for such sorrow paralyzes the soul, and hinders it from shunning evil."[100]

So what do you do when suffering becomes pathological?

At that point, you might be ready to consider treatment options. And one of those treatments might well involve medication.

This leads us to a direct consideration of antidepressant drugs.

---

[99] St. Thomas Aquinas, *ST*, I-II, q. 37, a. 3.
[100] Ibid., I-II, q. 39, a. 3.

10

Antidepressants

Notwithstanding everything I've said so far about the value of suffering, I hope I've made it abundantly clear in advance that I'm not going to rule out the potential benefits of using chemical treatment designed to counteract depression. I have no interest in condemning antidepressants wholesale.

That's because, as I ended the last chapter by pointing out, sorrow can become unhealthy. More specifically, one of the results of depression can be a disconnection between the person and the real world. And that's not a good place to be. Whenever a person's mental state is severed from the real world—whether due to drugs or due to sorrow—it's a problem.

So what do you do when suffering becomes disordered?

When Response Systems
Become Counterproductive

Since sorrow is the response to some perceived evil, and since depression is the response to some sorrow, I think it might be helpful to look at some analogies on the physical plane, i.e., systems in the human body that serve the purpose of responding to some threat but sometimes overreact in problematic ways.

HOW TO FEEL GOOD and HOW NOT TO

A first example: When my eldest son was about a year old, he woke up one morning with a temperature of 105 degrees. We raced him to the ER, where the staff gave him something to bring the fever down. The hospital doctor explained, though, that having *some* fever was good—a high temperature was the body's way of trying to burn out the infection, which was, of course, the root problem. The fever itself wasn't bad, but it had gotten out of control and needed to be brought back within healthy limits.

Here's another example: Some people are really allergic to poison ivy. Sometimes, after they've been exposed, rashes will still break out weeks later in new areas, even if the poison was all washed off long ago. So they get medicine, not to eliminate the poison (which is already gone), but to calm down the immune system, which is still in panic mode and still producing rashes. Again, the immune system is a good thing, and it does good work. It's just that in this case, it overreacts and needs to be chemically subdued.

A final example, this time in the area of physical pain: Suppose the side of my mouth hurts terribly, and I go to the dentist. The dentist checks things out, tells me he has found the infection, and we schedule a root canal. In the meantime, I get some pain meds, and on the day of the surgery, I'm given local anesthesia. Why? Because pain is bad? Not at all. In fact, pain was what alerted me to the problem and motivated me to do something about it in the first place. It served its proper function. But now the pain doesn't know I've taken the appropriate steps to heal the infection, and, in fact, if I don't get anesthetized, I won't be able to sit still during the surgery. Paradoxically, for the pain to achieve its purpose, it has to be neutralized.

This shows that good, useful response systems can become unbalanced and counterproductive. When that's the case, measures can be taken to get the system back under control.

Chemically Reducing Disordered Sorrow

Sorrow is a response system to evil, and like our other human systems, it can get off track. As we've seen, sorrow has a twofold purpose: first, to respond to perceived evil, and second, to motivate some improvement of the situation. Consequently, sorrow can be excessively disproportionate if it's too intense or if it inhibits improvement instead of prompting it.

Sorrow is disordered if it's too intense for the situation. For instance, college professors are usually anonymously evaluated by their students at the end of the semester. Suppose Professor Jones gets generally positive reviews from his students, but whenever he gets the rare negative review, he becomes sullen and joyless for an extended period. That would be disordered sorrow, because it's out of all proportion to the situation (they're just student evaluations, and he usually gets nice ones anyway). Something's wrong with *him* if that's how he reacts to just a little anonymous negative criticism.

Sorrow is also disordered if it prevents improvement of the situation. Suppose Mr. Smith is unexpectedly fired. He feels resentment and fear and confusion and just checks out. He almost never leaves the house, he orders takeout food for nearly every meal, and he spends his days watching TV and sleeping. That's bad news. His sorrow should be energizing him to find another job and maybe also causing him to reflect on how ultimate security doesn't exist in this life, but only in the next. Instead, his sorrow is crippling him, distracting him from both prayer and work prospects.

I think it wouldn't be controversial to label these cases as instances of disordered sorrow. Sorrow is a natural human faculty, but it's not supposed to look like this.

So the question is: Should Professor Jones and Mr. Smith be put on antidepressants?

I take it back. That's not the question. Not the question for me to answer, anyway. It's a prudential question, a question that has to be decided by these individuals, their therapists, and the relevant prescriber.

(Also, by the way, if you want to go off taking antidepressants, that has to be done carefully too, under the supervision of the relevant mental-health professional. Some of these medications have addictive qualities, and going cold-turkey can lead to devastating experiences of withdrawal.)

But those kinds of prudential decisions need to be made on a case-by-case basis. This chapter is about the general principles that should be kept in mind when trying to make a particular choice for a particular situation.

We've been over many of those principles already. We've seen that while sorrow is an appropriate response to evil, it can become disordered in various ways. There's no good reason why, in principle at least, it couldn't be useful to take drugs in order to reduce such disordered sorrow.

But we've also seen that there's no conclusive evidence indicating that these drugs are addressing the root cause of disordered sorrow, because as we've seen, there's no known neurological state that corresponds to depression in the first place.[101] That means that antidepressants should be used only insofar as they *facilitate* finding and treating the root cause of depression; they shouldn't be used as a *substitute* for finding and treating the problem.

Go back to the scenario with the dentist. Suppose when I go into the dentist complaining of pain in my mouth, the dentist just prescribes me some painkillers. He doesn't even look in my mouth. He just says, "Try these, and if the pain doesn't go away,

---

[101] Johann Hari, in his recent book, writes that the depression-as-brain-disease model is "lying broken on the floor, like a neurochemical Humpty Dumpty with a very sad smile." *Lost Connections: Uncovering the Real Causes of Depression — and the Unexpected Solutions* (London: Bloomsbury, 2019), 30.

let me know and we'll try a different medicine." That's no good. My pain means something—it's not just coming from nowhere. We need to find out what the problem is and how to fix it, and the pain medication is supposed to help us do that. It's not a solution by itself. And, by the way, once the problem *is* fixed, I should be able to go off the pain meds.

So, too, if antidepressant drugs are used in a given case of disordered sorrow, it should be only to make it easier to find and fix the cause of the disordered sorrow. In other words, these drugs can serve as an aid to therapy. Catholic psychiatrists Anna Terruwe and Conrad Baars make this point nicely:

> The psychiatrist must preserve the proper balance between primary and secondary treatment methods and guard against the danger of using secondary treatments, particularly pharmacological treatment, to the exclusion, or near exclusion, of primary psychotherapy. This danger is greatest when the case load of the psychiatrist is heaviest and time available for psychotherapy is limited. The remedy for this situation can never be more effective psychotropic drugs, for drugs themselves are never sufficient to heal disturbances caused by psychological factors.[102]

If the reason for the sorrow is in the soul, you're not going to take care of the problem by going after the body. Limiting yourself to a physical treatment for a spiritual ailment is missing the mark at a categorical level. It's like trying to fix a broken car with words of love and encouragement.

---

[102] Anna A. Terruwe and Conrad W. Baars, *Psychic Wholeness and Healing: Using ALL the Powers of the Human Psyche* (Staten Island, NY: Alba House, 1981), 127.

HOW TO FEEL GOOD and HOW NOT TO

Remember, it doesn't work to say that antidepressants are treating a brain disorder because we have no proof that depression is, in fact, caused by a brain disorder. There's not an apparent biological problem in depressed people's lives, but there's always a spiritual problem in depressed people's lives—because there's always a spiritual problem in *all* our lives. Error and sin and disappointment and wounds from our past threaten to overwhelm any of us at any given time.

Which spiritual problems in particular are depressed people responding to? I don't know. You'll have to talk to them. You'll have to get to know them. Is it a perspective problem? Is it a life-situation problem? Is it a moral problem? Some deep personal issues require deep personal reflection in order to get any insight. You don't just walk in, ask a few questions from a checklist or look at a scan, and then say, "Oh, I know what's wrong with you."

Spiritual problems are different from physical problems in another way too. With physical problems, sometimes you know what the problem is, but there's nothing you can do to fix it, nothing you can do even to make it better. Sometimes palliative care is all you can offer with an incurable or terminal illness. The only thing to do is ease the pain.

With complaints of the soul, that's not the case. There's always more that can be done for the soul—always growth in virtue, in fortitude, in love, and—as the Faith reminds us—in unity with the Cross of Christ. If someone sees no value in life, or in himself, it's never enough to shrug your shoulders and say, "Well, I give up. I don't know what the problem is. Here, just take these pills, and if they don't work, come back in and we'll try a different dose or a different medication." We can always do more for the soul than that.

In fact, it may well be that the culture of recreational drugs is partially fueled by the cultural trend of managing all feelings with chemicals. The Pontifical Council for Health Pastoral Care laments the general attitude in society that promotes the use of pharmaceutical products, under the pretext of medical assistance, to help people in difficulty live better, without however resolving their problems. From their youngest age, children are at the same time witnesses and object of these practices.... The child therefore learns very soon to face his or her moods and emotions by taking recourse to a pharmaceutical product.... Excessive use of medications by young people will, in the course of adolescence, stimulate them to search for other products, in order to regulate the crises that they face, and overcome the inevitable difficulties of life, rather than learn to check their affections on the basis of elements offered by the psychic life and the moral conscience.[103]

Again, antidepressant use isn't wrong in itself. It's a valid therapeutic option, a legitimate tool to help in the healing process. Persons *are* physical, we *are* embodied, and it makes sense that we would use material means in trying to get a handle on urgent mental issues.

Just don't treat depression as though it's only a physical problem. Emotional issues are never just a physical problem: a corpse might have a broken leg, but a corpse could never feel depressed. So when you're dealing with the passions of the soul, you don't want to limit your help to chemistry. Because people, and their personal problems, involve more than just chemicals.

Counteracting Sorrow

Not all extreme sorrow is dysfunctional. As we saw in the last chapter, many of the greatest saints went through periods of intense

---

[103] *Church: Drugs and Drug Addiction*, no. 249.

mental suffering, but it didn't interfere with their ability to live virtuously in service to God and neighbor. Nonetheless, as St. Francis de Sales observes, sorrow often leads to an attitude that is in tension with the life of a Christian:

> The "sorrow of the world" disturbs the heart, plunges it into anxiety, stirs up unreasonable fears, disgusts it with prayer, overwhelms and stupefies the brain, deprives the soul of wisdom, judgment, resolution, and courage, weakening all its powers; in a word, it is like a hard winter, blasting all the earth's beauty, and numbing all animal life; for it deprives the soul of sweetness and power in every faculty.[104]

De Sales consequently urges all to "vigorously resist all tendencies to melancholy, and although all you do may seem to be done coldly, wearily, and indifferently, do not give in." At the same time, he directs the Christian, "Resign yourself into God's Hands, endeavoring to bear this harassing depression patiently.... Above all, never doubt but that, after He has tried you sufficiently, God will deliver you from the trial."[105]

De Sales's advice to those dealing with overwhelming suffering is straightforward: do what you can to fight against depression, and in the meantime trust in God and be patient.

So, apart from seeking help from mental health professionals, how does one resist sorrow?

Aquinas's answer to that question is very clear: the way to counteract sorrow is with delight. Sorrow comes from experiencing evil, so of course its proper antidote involves experiencing good. The goods and evils don't even have to be in the same zone, since

---

[104] St. Francis de Sales, *Introduction to the Devout Life* (New York: Random House, 2002), 204–205.

[105] Ibid., 205–206.

a good in one aspect of human life can refocus attention away from an evil in a different aspect of human life: "so every pleasure brings relief by assuaging any kind of sorrow, due to any cause whatever."[106]

That means that goods of the body can help. Even a spiritual sorrow can be at least partially offset by a physical good. In fact, Aquinas mentions a number of physical "remedies" for sorrow. The first is tears, since crying is the natural physical activity proportionate to sorrow, and appropriate physical activities are good. Plus, crying is an outward expression of an interior state, so when a depressed person is locked in on himself, tears can reconnect him with the outside world.[107] Aquinas also mentions sleep, or even taking a hot bath, as a way of bringing the body back to its natural, and therefore pleasing, state.[108]

A disorder in the body can affect the soul. If you're not sleeping, if you're physically tensed up, if you don't exercise, if your diet is terrible — if this kind of stuff is going on, you don't need to blame your depression on psychological factors or a dark night of the soul. By the same token, a genuine good of the body — a good sleep or a good meal or a little exercise — can help you feel better psychologically.[109] Remember, we're not speculating about brain-chemical balances and imbalances here: we're talking about what's clearly bad for the body and what's clearly good for the body, and how the first can dampen and the second can raise your spirits.

But of course, in the long run, spiritual suffering can be outweighed only by spiritual delight. A trial to the soul is adequately counterbalanced only by an enjoyment proper to the soul. And

---

[106] *ST*, I-II, q. 38, a. 1.

[107] Ibid., a. 2.

[108] Ibid., a. 5.

[109] See St. Francis de Sales: "Moderate bodily discipline is useful in resisting depression, because it rouses the mind from dwelling on itself." *Devout Life*, 206.

HOW TO FEEL GOOD and HOW NOT TO

I've already devoted several chapters to how spiritual delight can be cultivated as a response to spiritual goods. There's delight in being (rest), delight in truth (contemplation), delight in others (community), and delight in order and surprise clothed in physical form (beauty).

We shouldn't try merely to get ourselves (or other people) *out* of depression. We should work at getting *into* these delights. Then the depression will have really been of great benefit, because it will have prompted a movement from less flourishing to more flourishing. It will have helped us reach what we were made for.

Part 4

Moral Conclusions

11

Drugs and the Purpose of the Soul

Mental Function and Psychological Health

It's very common when discussing mental issues to use the term "function." We call someone a "functioning alcoholic," or we ask how well someone can "function" on marijuana, or whether he can "function" without some kind of psychopharmaceutical medication. "Functioning" in this context usually seems to mean something such as holding down a job, paying bills on time, and not periodically erupting into screaming or violence.

The odd thing is that in other contexts the related word "functional" describes a thing that is capable of achieving the purpose for which it was made. A functional light bulb gives light, and a functional car can take you from one place to another. So it doesn't really make sense to talk about "functional" people unless you've got a clear grip on the purpose for which people were made. And surely the ultimate purpose of human life must involve more than maintaining a nine-to-five and resisting spasmodic behavior.

What's the ultimate purpose of human life? What's the ultimate goal? If we can't answer that question—or worse, if we think there isn't an answer—we'll just view our existence as a series of arbitrary, aimless firings, like an archer shooting arrows randomly at no target in particular. St. John Paul II says that this purposeless

view, this inability to find a stable goal for human existence, is
where drug abuse starts:

> Psychologists and sociologists say that the first cause that
> drives youth and adults to the harmful experience of drugs
> is a lack of clear and convincing motivations for life. In fact,
> the lack of points of reference, the vacuum of values, the
> conviction that nothing has sense and that life is not worth
> living, the tragic and distressing feeling of being unknown
> wayfarers in an absurd universe, can lead some to the search
> for a desperate and exasperated escape.[110]

The other term that gets thrown around in discussions about
psychological issues is "mental health." Now, the only way we
could make sense of physical health is if we understood the different parts of the body and what they're made to do. Likewise, the
only way to understand psychological health is to understand the
different parts of the soul and what *they're* made to do. Unless we
can commit to a view about these powers of the psyche and their
overall purpose, we can't even get close to figuring out what makes
a mind healthy or unhealthy:

> It is reasonable to assume that psychiatrists and others who
> like to call themselves "mental health professionals," when
> in a reflective mood, must be painfully aware of the irony
> that there exists no truly satisfying definition of "mental
> health." How many of them realize that there cannot be such
> a definition unless the spiritual dimension were included?
> Yet, if serious consideration were given to the existence and
> role of the spiritual powers of man, the profession would
> possess a clearer diagnostic criterion and therapeutic goal

---

[110] Homily at a Mass for ex–drug addicts, August 9, 1980.

to aid it in promoting what then would better be called "psychic wholeness."[111]

We can't know what it means to be psychologically functional, and we can't know what it means to be psychologically healthy, unless we're clear on the different capacities in the soul—what they are and what they're for.

What are the powers of the psyche? They are traditionally thought of as the *intellect*, the *will*, and the *passions*. This book has dealt throughout with the passions, but the passions themselves get their moral significance from the intellect and the will. And *those* powers, in turn, exist to enable us to engage with reality.

Reality and the Soul

Just as food is the proper object of the stomach, and air is the proper object of the lungs, so reality, or being, is the proper object of the intellect and the will, such that unless the soul is nourished by reality, it starves and asphyxiates.

Like the senses, the different powers of our soul are pointed *outward*. We are designed to engage with things beyond ourselves. And just as the senses allow us to engage with different aspects of physical reality, so do the powers of the soul allow us to engage with different aspects of ultimate reality.

Take the intellect. Reality as the object of the intellect is called *truth*. This is how the mind is supposed to work, by conforming itself to reality.[112]

---

[111] Conrad Baars, introduction to Terruwe and Baars, *Psychic Wholeness and Healing*, viii.

[112] The mind can also know unreal things (e.g., a talking rabbit and tortoise that decide to race), but it's fulfilled by such knowledge only insofar as knowing the fictional thing gives insight into the

HOW TO FEEL GOOD and HOW NOT TO

Of course, that presupposes that there exists some objective reality to which the mind can conform itself. But there is an objective reality, and everyone knows it. Nobody ever says reality or truth is subjective when it has to do with something they care about. Football fans never say that it's a matter of opinion who was declared the winner of last year's Super Bowl. Tax auditors never say it's up to you to decide whether you think you make fifty thousand a year or a hundred thousand a year. Scientists never say it's subjective whether the earth is round or flat. Women's advocacy groups never say the morality of violence against women is a matter of private conviction. People say that everything is relative only when they want to be intellectually lazy or indifferent. They say there's no object for the intellect only when they don't want to use their intellects at all.

One of the easiest ways to prove the existence of an objective reality beyond the mind is the fact that we argue with each other. Everyone knows we can't argue about private experience. If you tell me about a dream you had, there's no way for me to argue with you about it—I had no access to what you saw or felt in your dream. So, if we were all just living in our own private dream worlds, no argument could have ever gotten started. The reason we can and do disagree about things is that there's a reality outside our minds, to which we all have access, and to which we appeal as a standard of accuracy, of truth.

And if reality as it pertains to the intellect is called *truth*, so reality as the proper object of the will is called *good*.

---

real world (e.g., slow but steady wins the race). That's why, for instance, indulgence in fantasy can become so unhealthy when it leads its consumers further and further from engagement with reality.

We would normally say that something is good insofar as it fulfills its design, or the purpose of its nature; this suggests that what holds for the word "functional" also holds for the word "good." A pen is a good pen if it writes clearly and easily; a flashlight is a good flashlight if it provides sufficient light reliably. If the flashlight gives only sketchy light, or the pen spills ink sloppily, we'd say it's not a very good flashlight or a good pen, because it doesn't function rightly.

Human beings have a specific nature as well, and it's a very complicated nature, such that it's fulfilled in a variety of ways. We are fulfilled by food, by drink, by friendship, by sexual intimacy, by knowledge, by beauty, and so forth. So we would say that all these things—all these realities—are "good" for us, because they help us to become fulfilled; i.e., they perfect us and so, in a certain sense, make us good people.

Consequently, things are "goods" when they help us become "good" (that is to say, when they fulfill us). This is the proper object of the will: realities that are good or complete in themselves and enable us to become good or complete.

In sum, reality is the proper goal of the intellect as truth and the proper goal of the will as goodness. But what is the ultimate reality? What is the source of reality and, therefore, of all truth and goodness? What is pure reality, Being Itself?

God is. God is He Who Is, the source of being and, by implication, the source of all truth and goodness. Created things are really true and good because they receive their dependent being from the Necessary Being. This is why following the trail of created goods and truths leads to God, just as following water upstream will eventually take you to the original spring.

That's why it's okay to pursue these intermediate, created truths and goods—because they're genuinely true and good and even fulfilling in their own limited way—but we're supposed to pursue them in such a way that it leads us toward the ultimate Truth and Good, toward that God who alone can give unending nourishment to the soul. "Whoever drinks the water I will give will never be thirsty again" (see John 4:14). It's sort of like the relationship between my job and my family. I like my job, it's a good job, but I should pursue it only to the extent that it serves my family; I'd better not put my job above my wife and kids. Likewise, we should pursue created things, but in such a way that it leads us closer to and not further from union with the Lord.

The intellect and the will, then, are made for truth and goodness and, ultimately, for God. That's our purpose. So, if you intentionally damage your intellect and your will, *you're attacking your capacity for God.*

That's why drunkenness, for instance, is such a huge deal. Getting drunk dulls the mind and weakens the will; it makes it harder for us to engage reality, and so makes it harder to seek the Source of all reality. It can cut us off from God; this is why we say drunkenness is grave matter—i.e., it has the potential to frustrate our ultimate destiny. St. Paul warns that drunkards will not inherit the kingdom of God (1 Cor. 6:10), which makes sense, since they've deliberately mutilated their capacity to know and love God.

And what's true of drunkenness is true of any drug use designed to compromise intelligence and freedom. The evil of drug abuse isn't primarily about the damage it does to the body or to social position. It's about how it can warp the soul and permanently render it incapable of fulfillment. Every such use of drugs is a divorce from reality and a frustration of the human person:

> The unreal character of this form of pleasure-seeking contradicts objective necessity and opposes the principle of reality. The pleasure-seeking is in radical conflict with the principle

of reality, which is the principle regulator, balancing all the forces at work: the subjective interests of the individual, the demands of reality, the vital needs of the individual, and the moral rules.[113]

The standard for mental health, the standard for psychological functioning, has to be reality itself and whether a given behavior or treatment causes you to engage it more or less fully. That's the fundamental human, the fundamental moral, criterion for evaluating the use of any psychoactive drug.

Responding to the Truth and Motivating Pursuit of the Good

Now let's bring together this understanding of our intellect, which is made to respond to reality, and our will, which is made to respond to reality, with an understanding of the passions—which, you guessed it, are also made to respond to reality. Our emotions, in fact, are designed to engage reality *precisely through the intellect and the will.* Our feelings should, when properly functioning:

1. Respond to the truth perceived by the intellect
2. Motivate the will to choose the good

That's it. That's what our feelings are designed to do. They're situated between intellect and will, and they're supposed to originate from the first and prompt a right exercise of the second. That's where the morality of the passions comes from. "In themselves passions are neither good nor evil. They are morally qualified only to the extent that they effectively engage reason and will."[114]

---

[113] Pontifical Council for Health Pastoral Care, *Church: Drugs and Drug Addiction*, 61.
[114] CCC 1767.

HOW TO FEEL GOOD and HOW NOT TO

This means there are two ways in which the natural purposes of our passions can be frustrated.

Our feelings are thwarted, first of all, when our intellects and wills don't do their jobs. If we don't know the truth, our passions will respond to a faulty picture of reality. If you have a wrong perception of things, your feelings will be correspondingly imbalanced. If a kid thinks there's a monster hiding under his bed, he'll be too scared to sleep — even though there's actually nothing to be scared of. By the same token, if you think the world is a brutal, senseless place, or if you think you yourself are worthless, you're going to feel pretty lousy about everything — even though you shouldn't.

Something similar happens when you live viciously. The passions are meant to propel us to will the good, as we've seen. So if you don't choose well, if you're constantly making bad choices, the passions won't be reaching their goal. In fact, if your will is consistently directed the wrong way, your passions will become similarly deformed.

If the emotion is good, but the will resists the good impulse for long enough, then the emotion itself will eventually bend to evil as well. Do something bad enough, and you'll get used to it, and then you'll get to like it, and then you'll get to need it. And at that point, your emotional life will be all out of joint.

So, if the intellect and the will go wrong, the passions will be damaged in both their origin and their direction. But the other way the passions can be frustrated is *if they are separated from the intellect and the will* — that is, if the passions are no longer responding to perception, and if they're no longer motivating the will. A workhorse's job is to follow the reins and pull the cart; if it shakes free of its bridle and harness and runs wild, it is no longer fulfilling its function. By the same token, if a person takes drugs in order to let his feelings enjoy themselves, regardless of what the person's thoughts and choices are, his feelings will be set adrift from the only anchors that can give them stability and meaning.[115]

Okay, here are the implications of all this talk about proper emotional functioning:

Ethics is about people working the way they're designed to work. In other words, as we just saw, "good," in a moral context, means people functioning the way they're supposed to.

A good feeling, for example, is a response to reality as you accurately perceive it to be. For instance, if something's really wrong, and you feel bad about it, that's a good feeling to have. And if something's really right, and you know it's right, and your knowledge causes you to feel good, that's a good feeling too.

But the corollary is that moral evil is any action that frustrates proper human functioning. If you are deliberately doing something that frustrates or opposes the way your soul is supposed to work, it's a moral evil.

So, if you're trying to stimulate your emotions to respond to things they're not designed to respond to—e.g., artificial chemical interventions that affect your feelings independently of intellect and will—then that's not morally okay. That's a disordered feeling, and you shouldn't deliberately try to make yourself feel something disordered.

Whereas if you have a feeling that's already disordered—say, a disproportionate level of sadness—and you take a drug to try to get the sorrow under control, that wouldn't be violating the soul's connection to reality. The soul would be *already* out of touch with reality, and the medication would be part of an effort to neutralize that unrealistic feeling.

---

[115] Remember, too, that a horse's relationship to the bridle and harness is artificial, whereas it belongs to the intrinsic purpose of the passions to be engaged with reason and will.

There are, then, three ways to use a mood-altering substance relative to reality:

1. As a substitute for reality, which involves stimulating feelings independently of their proper real-world objects
2. As a celebration of reality, which means using the substance otherwise than as a drug
3. As a (partial) antidote to feelings that are already disparate to reality, which means using the substance to overcome disordered emotions

These three uses don't correspond exactly to marijuana, alcohol, and antidepressants. But it's understanding the different moral values of these three uses that will allow us to supply moral principles that should govern our use of these three substances. We'll elaborate these principles explicitly in the following—and final—chapter.

12

Which Drugs Am I Allowed to Take?

When it comes to controversial ethical issues, someone might be looking for quick answers to simple questions. You might, for instance, have been hoping for quick Q & A–type answers to the following questions:

"Is it okay to smoke marijuana?"

"How about eating weed brownies?"

"Is there anything wrong with taking antidepressants?"

"How many beers is too many beers?"

But none of these questions is well formulated enough to answer clearly. The reason is that all these questions focus on the *substance* instead of on the *use*. And when you're looking at ethical issues, it's not enough to look at the physical ingredients involved. You have to look at the nature of the act. In other words, you have to examine *what* you are trying to do.

What Are You Trying to Do?

What is the first step in moral evaluation? If you want to try to figure out whether it's morally legitimate to make a certain choice, what is the first question you should ask yourself?

It may sound obvious, but the first thing to look at is, again, *what* you're trying to do. And, as a matter of fact, a lot of people—even a lot of ethical theorists—forget to ask this question. They ask about motivations, and likely outcomes, and the specifics of the given situation, but they don't take the time carefully to examine the nature of the act they're considering.

In the Catholic moral tradition, an act's nature is called its "object." The moral object is what you are trying to do. To reiterate, it's *the nature of the act chosen by the agent.* And, morally and even logically speaking, this comes first. Before you can talk about why, or where, or when, or how, or under what conditions, you need to be clear on *what.* And the *what* of an act is its object.

The problem is that figuring out the nature of an act isn't always easy. Two acts that look the same on the surface may actually be very different—so different, in fact, that one act might be evil while the other one is good (or at least neutral). So we want to be very careful at this most elementary stage of moral evaluation, to avoid the temptation of mixing up objects and lumping together actions with very different structures and characters.

There is, moreover, a key principle that guards against confusion regarding the moral object—namely, *an act's nature is NOT equivalent to the act's material aspect.* Human beings are a composite of spiritual and material components, and so are our actions. Two behaviors could look the same physically but have different intrinsic natures. Fornication and marital consummation have the same material manifestations, they may superficially look the same, but they don't have the same nature, which is evident when we realize that one is always morally bad, and the other is, considered in itself, morally good. In this case, the state of being married isn't some factor extrinsic to the act: its presence or absence determines what kind of act is being committed. The implication is that "sexual behavior" isn't a full human act, but rather a physical component of certain acts whose overall character depends on further human factors.

Take another example, and one closer to our topic: the birth-control pill. If a woman takes the pill to sterilize her sexual behaviors, she's choosing to contracept; whereas if she's not sexually active and is taking the pill to regulate her cycle, she's making a medical choice. Again, since it's the same substance that's consumed, the act appears identical from the empirical point of view, but morally speaking, different decisions are made in both cases.

So, too, the different substances we've talked about in this book could be used in different ways, which is why I've focused not so much on the chemical properties of the various drugs, but on the objects, that is, on *what people are trying to do* with these drugs. It seems to me that there's an enormous moral difference between taking a substance for the sake of:

- *Emotional manipulation*—in which the goal of the act is to stimulate enjoyment by altering the brain
- *Emotional therapy*—in which the goal of the act is to reduce sorrow by altering the brain
- *Appreciative enjoyment*—in which the goal of the act is to delight in the objective goodness of what is being consumed[116]

Antidepressants are generally associated with emotional therapy, and recreational cannabis is by definition associated with stimulating enjoyment. I've also argued that people commonly relate to alcoholic

---

[116] The "goal of the act" (*finis operis* in Latin) is another way of talking about the moral object, or *what* a person is trying to do. This is different from the "goal of the agent" (*finis operantis*), or the "end," which is *why* the person is doing what he's doing. For the purpose of our discussion, the end, or motivation of the person, is probably the same—or at least sufficiently similar—in all three cases: the person wants to feel better. This is a fine motivation, but as I've pointed out, it's important to look first at *what* he's choosing to do in order to achieve that end.

drinks in the third way — that is, they recognize it as something nutritious, hydrating, and excellent and appreciate it as such.

But as we just showed in the case of the birth-control pill, ingesting the same substance can be a different moral act depending on what you're trying to do. Certainly, alcohol and cannabis could be used for emotional therapy, and drugs normally prescribed for depression could be passed around and consumed indiscriminately at a college party or a nightclub. I can't imagine antidepressant pills ever being used for appreciative enjoyment, but certainly some recreational pot smokers combine a savoring of the taste and quality of the marijuana with the desire to get high.

The point, though, is not to become fixated on the moral property of the chemical itself. Chemicals are chemicals — they aren't morally good or evil except in particular contexts. They will be physically unhealthy to the extent that they do damage to the body, and they will be morally unhealthy to the extent that the person using them is knowingly trying to do something contrary to human flourishing.[117]

We also can't simply look at the material, superficially accessible state of the drug users. It's not enough to look at the physiological effects of the drugs, or the income levels associated with different classes of drug users, or the life-satisfaction ratings drug takers report. None of this can tell us whether or in what way it's morally acceptable to take the drugs in question. It tells us what happens or tends to happen under certain conditions, but not what *ought to* happen.

The only way we can know whether something is a worthy object of human choice is by looking at the whole human person — body

---

[117] "What is undoubtedly decisive in the approach to the problems of drug consumption, and has to be drawn to the attention of educators, is not only the quality of the products that are sought, but also the motivations that lead individuals to consume them." Pontifical Council for Health Pastoral Care, *Church: Drugs and Drug Addiction*, no. 167.

and soul—and its ultimate purpose. That's the ethical standard by which to judge different varieties of drug use.

Morally Legitimate and Morally Illegitimate Uses of Mood-Altering Drugs

We'll begin with recreational drug use, which, again, means attempting to get enjoyment by stimulating the brain, instead of seeking delight by attaining the goods for which our human faculties were designed. Consequently, recreational drug use means *targeting the brain in order to produce disordered delight*. Such a practice is immoral, plain and simple, for two reasons:

1. It is an abuse of the emotional faculties. Our good feelings were meant to originate from the presence of a perceived good, not from a brain disruption. To make our feelings respond to something they weren't designed for means *to act against our own design*, and that's exactly what is meant by moral perversion.

2. It saps our motivation to pursue the goods our emotions *are* designed to respond to. Pornography and masturbation are abuses of the sexual power, but they also dissipate the urge to pursue the good of marital intimacy for which the sexual power was designed. So, too, the false contentment recreational drug users feel encourages them to be satisfied with less than what they were made for: truth, love, beauty, and ultimately the joy of divine love.

John Paul II neatly summarized both these evils in the following appeal to the youth of the world:

> The use of drugs, on the contrary, is always illicit, since it involves an unjustifiable and irrational refusal to think, will and act as a human person.... One ought not to speak of

the "liberty to take drugs," or the "right to drugs," because the human being does not have the right to damage himself, nor should he ever abdicate the personal dignity that is his and that comes from God! We must always remember that these phenomena not only compromise physical and psychological well-being, but frustrate the person himself in his capacity for relationship and gift.... Guard yourselves from the temptations to certain tragic and illusory experiences! Don't give in to them! Why start down a dead-end road? Why reject the full maturity of your years, in favor of a premature senility? Why squander your lives and your energies, which might instead be used to discover a joyous affirmation of the ideals of honesty, of work, of sacrifice, of purity, of genuine love?[118]

It's morally wrong to use *any* drug to produce disordered delight —artificial delight responding to chemical interventions instead of responding to the proper goods of body and soul. Marijuana is largely consumed in this context, and there are probably plenty of cases where alcohol is misused the same way. Recall from the previous chapter that our feelings are supposed to respond to perception, and in particular to the intellect. Consequently, if a given substance compromises the functioning of the intellect and other perceptive faculties, then to the extent that the drug's chemical psychoagency is operative, it will preclude, not promote, virtuous delight.

Certainly, the cannabis plant as a substance isn't evil, and it has other uses besides emotional recreation. You might be able to use it medicinally, to heal certain physical conditions, as a painkiller

---

[118] St. John Paul II, Address to the Participants at the International Conference on Drugs and Alcohol, November 23, 1991, no. 4, translation mine.

in the case of intense pain, or before bed as an anti-insomnia treatment. These uses might entail certain risks, and there are prudential factors to consider—many of which are debated even among specialists—but certainly if these were the users' sincere goals, such employment of the plant wouldn't fall under the same moral condemnation as recreational drug use.

So what about cannabis used for emotionally therapeutic reasons?

I don't know how safe or effective marijuana is for treating depression, and I've talked to enough clinicians to know that they disagree among themselves. But there's definitely an enormous difference, morally speaking, between using a drug to produce disordered delight (drug use for emotional recreation) and using a drug to reduce disordered sorrow (drug use for emotional therapy).

This latter kind of drug use, therapeutic drug use, is precisely the kind of use for which antidepressant medications are prescribed in standard practice. There doesn't seem to be anything intrinsically wrong with this kind of use, as recent magisterial sources have confirmed.

For instance, St. John Paul II stated that "recourse to tranquilizing substances on medical advice in order to alleviate—in well-defined cases—physical and psychological suffering should be governed by very prudent criteria in order to offset dangerous forms of addiction and dependence."[119]

In 1995, the Pontifical Council for Pastoral Assistance took a similar position: "Administered for therapeutic purposes and with due respect for the person, psychopharmaceuticals are ethically legitimate."[120]

---

[119] Ibid., as translated in *Charter for Healthcare Workers*, no. 101.
[120] *Charter for Healthcare Workers*, no. 102.

HOW TO FEEL GOOD and HOW NOT TO

The *Catechism* says that the use of drugs, "except on therapeutic grounds," is seriously sinful (no. 2291), which seems to suggest that drug use on therapeutic grounds can be morally licit.

Finally, in 2001, the Pontifical Council for Health Pastoral Care affirmed that "the consumption of psychotropic medicines" can be "necessary in the state of depression and other abnormalities."[121]

Such drug use may involve moral risks, but not moral transgressions. In other words, one would have to be careful not to dismiss suffering and sorrow as morally irrelevant—which could happen in the case of overzealous medicating of emotional issues—but there wouldn't be anything unethical about trying to use drugs as part of a program to get the emotions back within certain healthy limits.

Lastly, appreciative enjoyment. Alcoholic drinks, as we've said all along, aren't without their serious moral dangers. Deliberate drunkenness, for instance, is a grave sin, since it inhibits the intellect's capacity for truth and the will's capacity for free pursuit of the good. Furthermore, since (as I pointed out in the last chapter), God is the ultimate end of the intellect and the will, warping these faculties inhibits our capacity to engage God Himself. Thus, in Aquinas's words:

> With regard to drunkenness we reply that it is a mortal sin by reason of its genus; for, that a man, without necessity, and through the mere lust of wine, make himself unable to use his reason, whereby he is directed to God and avoids committing many sins, is expressly contrary to virtue.[122]

Moreover, when we drink *in order to* alter our mental state chemically, we are attempting to drug ourselves with alcohol:

---

[121] *Church: Drugs and Drug Addiction*, no. 177.
[122] *ST*, I-II, q. 88, a. 5.

Alcoholic drunkenness is as much a danger and could provoke in dependent individuals serious disorders like loss of vigilance, of moral sense, of self-control and also the development of aggressive and violent attitudes, the tendency to estrange oneself from reality, psychopathological problems, liver diseases, etc. In many societies, wine and alcohol form part of dining; obviously, *since these products are not completely free from dangers, they can become drugs*, provoking serious illnesses and very high rates of mortality.[123]

But when we consume alcoholic beverages to nourish, hydrate, and delight ourselves with something excellently made, we are using these drinks in a genuinely recreational way — and not as a drug at all. In the words of St. John Paul II: "*There exists, certainly, a definite difference between use of drugs and the use of alcohol:* while the moderate use of the first as a drink does not violate moral norms, and hence only its abuse is to be condemned, the use of drugs, on the contrary, is always illicit."[124]

One needn't desire beer, wine, or spirits for their psychoactive properties. One may desire them as one instance (admittedly among many) of the beauty the world offers for our appreciative enjoyment. In such a case, drinking avoids violating moral norms and can serve moreover as an opportunity for edification.

The Primary Moral Issue

I'm well aware that this book hasn't addressed nearly all the ethically relevant issues at stake in the case of mood-altering drugs.

---

[123] Pontifical Council for Health Pastoral Care, *Church: Drugs and Drug Addiction*, no. 166, emphasis mine.

[124] St. John Paul II, Address to the Participants at the International Conference on Drugs and Alcohol, no. 4, translation mine.

HOW TO FEEL GOOD and HOW NOT TO

For instance: How effective are the drugs, and to what extent do the drug effects vary across different users? How addictive are the drugs? What are the best strategies for overcoming addiction? What physiological side effects are there? What psychological side effects are there? Does the government have a role? If it does have a role, should it be one of prohibition or regulation? If taking certain drugs is wrong, how gravely wrong is it, and how culpable are drug users, producers, and distributors? How much of a person's response to a given substance is traceable to the placebo effect? How practically important is the distinction between organic and synthetic drugs? What role should professional therapists play?

These are all important moral issues, but they aren't the main moral issue.

People are taking drugs to feel good and to stop feeling bad. They're doing it more and more. It's becoming increasingly legal and increasingly normalized, but that doesn't mean it's a good thing.

The only way to tell if the ingestion of a chemical is a good thing is to see how we're made, and what we're made for.

We're made for real goodness. Our faculties are built to pursue and delight in the intermediate goodness of the created world, and the supreme goodness of the Uncreated God. Only acts geared toward an increased emotional engagement with reality — not decreased engagement — are suited to our nature as intelligent, free creatures, made in the image and likeness of God, and called to perfection.[125]

---

[125] "All the faithful, whatever their condition or state, are called by the Lord, each in his own way, to that perfect holiness whereby the Father Himself is perfect." Second Vatican Council, Dogmatic Constitution on the Church *Lumen gentium* (November 21, 1964), no. 11:

Conclusion

"They Have No Wine": The Joy and Sorrow of the Mother of God

I want to end this book by allowing Our Lady to illustrate the principles gleaned in the course of the preceding chapters. Mary is the Christian model, our exemplar in every aspect of faith and experience. Mary is the perfect disciple, the perfect human being. Her life should consequently manifest a perfect pattern of delight and sorrow.

Begin with delight. We've affirmed, over and over, that delight involves rest in a present perceived good and that it involves an attitude of receptivity, of *being* over *doing*. Mary manifests that. She hardly ever *does* anything in the New Testament. She doesn't preach or work miracles or minister to the poor or baptize or administer. But she receives the gifts of God; better, she supremely receives the supreme gift of God. It's exactly her reception, her willing acceptance of God's will and God's Son that constitutes her greatest achievement.

An attitude of rest allows for a contemplation of truth, truth about the greatness of God, the greatness of what He has done, and our own littleness, all of which culminates in a pervasive outlook of gratitude. Mary manifests that. She has the habit of pondering in her heart, which is to say that she has the habit of contemplating what matters most. The result is expressed in the grateful exclamations of the Magnificat, where, in a few words, she celebrates God's greatness and generosity and her own relative inconsequence:

> My soul proclaims the greatness of the Lord;
> My spirit rejoices in God my savior.
> For he has looked upon his handmaid's lowliness;
> Behold, from now on will all ages call me blessed,
> The Mighty One has done great things for me.
> (Luke 1:46–49)

Mary knows how to be happy, and she is the ideal instructor in the art of Christian delight: "She has grasped, better than all other creatures, that God accomplishes wonderful things.... And it is with good reason that her children on earth, turning to her who is the mother of hope and of grace, invoke her as the cause of their joy."[126]

I don't think many Catholics have thought much about Mary as the model for delight—but most of us are familiar with the Mater Dolorosa. We've seen her supreme moment of agony captured in one of the many artistic expressions of the pietà. We know that Mary knew sorrow.

In addition to the potential benefits for the sufferer, Christians know that God used suffering as the currency to save the world. More than that, as His disciples, we are all called to "make up what is lacking in the sufferings of Christ," as Paul says (Col. 1:24). And Mary was the first Christian to do that. Simeon told her in advance; he prophesied that her heart would be pierced. And yet nowhere in Scripture do we read that she was actually, physically pierced.

Who was physically pierced? Jesus was. Did it hurt Him, did it cause Him to suffer, when the soldier's lance stabbed through the

---

[126] Paul VI, *Gaudete in Domino*, no. 4.

flesh and started the spray of blood and water? No, Jesus didn't feel it. Remember? He was already dead. He couldn't hurt anymore. He had already cried out, "It is finished." His work of saving the world through suffering was over.

But someone else felt that wound. For Mary, the torture continued when the Lord's body was subject to one more cruel and atrocious mutilation. She responded with due horror and agony to that final gratuitous violation—that evil—on Golgotha. Mary suffered from Jesus' final injuries even when Jesus didn't. Mary made up what was lacking in the sufferings of Christ before they even took Him off the Cross.

So she can be our model for delight, and she can be our model for sorrow.

And she does more than model. She intercedes.

Let's finish by looking one more time at a potentially mood-altering chemical: wine. We've seen that wine is a good, and one that the Psalms tell us can be a source of delight that "gladdens man's heart."

On the day of Pentecost, when the Apostles were filled with the Spirit and with zeal, the cynics said, "They are filled with new wine" (Acts 2:13, RSCVE). They meant to accuse the proclaimers and hearers of the Gospel of being drunkards, but their vicious slur turned into a witness to the truth. Our Lord Himself had described the Gospel as the New Wine when He said "New Wine is for New Wineskins" (see Luke 5:38), and now the Apostles, who represented the New Wineskin of the Church, had been filled with the New Joy—the New Wine—of the Resurrection.

Those of us who are members of the Church, who believe in God's love and a Savior and the prospect of eternal bliss—we ought to be the most obviously cheerful, happy people out there. But often enough we aren't. We struggle with the same ennui, the same malaise, the same sluggish spirit as everyone else.

HOW TO FEEL GOOD and HOW NOT TO

When we feel like this, our first recourse should be to the Mother of God. And we should tell her that our hearts are heavy, that our spirits are depressed, that we're running low on delight, on the New Wine of the Gospel. And she will turn to the King, and she'll tell Him again what she told Him so long ago: "They have no wine." And He, who refuses His Mother nothing, will again work His miracle, and again His disciples will celebrate.

Acknowledgments

For starters, thanks to all the folks at Sophia who worked to put out and promote my previous book on beauty and who then invited the submission of the present volume, especially Jose Gonzalez, John Barger, Molly Rublee, Sarah Lemieux, and Charlie McKinney.

Thanks next to the people who prompted or supported my original dissertation on antidepressant drugs: Matthew Boudway, Joseph Thompson, Tony Salinski, Jeff Gainey, and in particular my dissertation advisor, Thomas D. Williams.

Thanks very much to the people who took the time to discuss the project: Luis Vera, Josh Hochschild, and Tikhon Pino, and to those who looked over the manuscript: Ellie Legare, Charlotte Ostermann, Sr. Marysia Weber, Owen Phelan, Greg Bottaro, and David Shields. Between the different viewpoints you all offered, I felt that I got an amazingly well-rounded perspective and a clear preview of likely reader responses. (I hasten to add that the gracious help of the above-mentioned doesn't constitute some kind of blanket endorsement of everything in the book. The views I offer are just mine.)

Special thanks goes to Mike Scherschligt, who discussed every chapter with me in detail as I was writing it, and lectured on the material to different groups—giving invaluable feedback.

Thanks, as always, to Jess, who was really encouraging and involved with this book, and to the kids.

And thanks in a special way to my siblings: Michael, Maria, Mariana, Joseph, Annaleah, Bernadette, and Philumena. You guys have always been so generous and encouraging over the years. I'd like to dedicate this book to you.

Sophia Institute

Sophia Institute is a nonprofit institution that seeks to nurture the spiritual, moral, and cultural life of souls and to spread the Gospel of Christ in conformity with the authentic teachings of the Roman Catholic Church.

Sophia Institute Press fulfills this mission by offering translations, reprints, and new publications that afford readers a rich source of the enduring wisdom of mankind.

Sophia Institute also operates the popular online resource CatholicExchange.com. *Catholic Exchange* provides world news from a Catholic perspective as well as daily devotionals and articles that will help readers to grow in holiness and live a life consistent with the teachings of the Church.

In 2013, Sophia Institute launched Sophia Institute for Teachers to renew and rebuild Catholic culture through service to Catholic education. With the goal of nurturing the spiritual, moral, and cultural life of souls, and an abiding respect for the role and work of teachers, we strive to provide materials and programs that are at once enlightening to the mind and ennobling to the heart; faithful and complete, as well as useful and practical.

Sophia Institute gratefully recognizes the Solidarity Association for preserving and encouraging the growth of our apostolate over the course of many years. Without their generous and timely support, this book would not be in your hands.

www.SophiaInstitute.com
www.CatholicExchange.com
www.SophiaInstituteforTeachers.org